Recovery of Local Overhead Incurred in Federal Grants

Recovery of Local Overhead Incurred in Federal Grants

James E. Kirk

Bureau of Governmental Research and Service
University of South Carolina

A Ronald Press Publication

John Wiley & Sons

New York · Chichester · Brisbane · Toronto

A Ronald Press Publication

Copyright © 1980 by John Wiley & Sons, Inc.

Library of Congress Cataloging in Publication Data
Kirk, James Edgar, 1948-
    Recovery of local overhead incurred in Federal
grants.

    "A Ronald Press publication."
    Includes index.
    1. Grants-in-aid—United States. 2. Local
finance—United States. I. Title.

HJ275.K57   350.72'5'0973   80-11771
ISBN 0-471-05914-5

Printed in the United States of America

10 9 8 7 6 5 4 3 2 1

Preface

It is common knowledge among local government officials that federal funds are not free. After grant programs have been terminated, local and state monies often take over the program operations. In addition, the contributions by the local unit of government during the federal program's operation are significant. These contributions often include the following:

1   The local government provides building space and equipment for the grant-funded employees.
2   The payroll clerk processes grant-funded employees' paychecks and fringe benefits and maintains their personnel files.

3   The chief administrator provides overall supervision of grant programs and oversees the grant application and financial reporting activities.

4   The clerk-treasurer or other finance officer maintains internal accounting records on grant expenditures and revenues and prepares financial reports to federal and state agencies.

5   The local government maintains and operates the vehicles used by grant employees.

This guide describes in detail a method for local governments to recover from the federal government some of these overhead costs that are often unnecessarily absorbed by the jurisdictions. The recovery involves the preparation of an "indirect cost allocation plan," which yields one or more indirect cost (overhead) rates for the jurisdiction. After approval by a federal agency, the overhead rate is then applied to grant reimbursement requests, and the overhead costs are reimbursed, along with the direct program costs. A jurisdiction's use of indirect cost rates on grants permits the federal government to share in the funding of supportive services, thereby decreasing the pressure on the property tax and other local revenues.

This guide is useful for nearly all local governmental units—cities, counties, special purpose districts, school districts, and regional councils of government. Although this guide focuses on local government's recovery of overhead, most of the principles and procedures described herein also apply to state government agencies. Thus the short form plan preparation method described in Chapter 4 is designed for use by local jurisdictions, while the method detailed in chapters 5 and 6 is applicable to all jurisdictions.

Chapter 1 introduces the cost allocation plans by explaining some of the terms and concepts and describing the benefits to local governments from preparation of plans. Chapter 2 describes the plan approval process, along with the procedures for applying approved overhead rates to federal grants. Chapter 3 presents a preview of the two optional methods of plan preparation and the factors local officials must consider in choosing one method over the other. These first three chapters are presented in a question-and-answer format for the convenience of the reader. The final four chapters, the bulk of the guide, explain step by step how cost allocation plans and indirect cost rate proposals are prepared. Chapter 4 details the consolidated, simplified method, which may be adequate for many small local governments. This chapter, along with the next two, uses extensive examples from local government plans. Chapters 5 and 6 describe the long form method, which yields the maximum recovery and takes considerably more time to complete than the simplified method. The final chapter summarizes the plan preparation process and highlights the contents of the final submission to the federal agency.

Users of this publication are encouraged to refer to the federal brochure on preparing indirect cost plans entitled *A Guide for State and Local Governments: Cost Principles and Procedures for Establishing Cost Allocation Plans and Indirect Cost Rates for Grants and Contracts with the Federal Government* (OASC–10).* This brochure includes the Office of Management and Budget's Federal Management Circular 74-4, "Cost Principles Applicable to Grants and Contracts with State and Local Governments." References to the federal brochure are included in all seven chapters of this guide, noted by the publication number "OASC–10," to enable local officials to make their own interpretation of the federal guidelines. The federal brochure and this guide apply to all units of local government—municipalities, counties, special purpose districts, and school districts—as well as to state governments.

JAMES E. KIRK

Columbia, South Carolina
February 1980

* Published in 1976 by the Department of Health, Education and Welfare (HEW) for application to all federal agency grants. It may be obtained from the Superintendent of Documents or HEW's Office of the Secretary.

Acknowledgments

I acknowledge the assistance of those individuals who contributed to the preparation of this guide. Several South Carolina local officials were especially helpful throughout the preparation of this guide in reviewing the drafts and assisting with the examples: Wayne Plylar and Barry Hickman of Spartanburg, Sterling Cheatham of Greenville, and Lewis Hudgins of Charleston. George Oliver, the state of South Carolina's Grants Service Administrator, and Robert Scott of the Manpower Division of the Governor's Office, also provided useful reviews of early drafts.

Comments from the following federal officials greatly assisted in assuring consistency with federal policies and procedures:

Rex Allred, Director, Division of Cost Allocations, Department of Health, Education, and Welfare, Region IV.

Fred Edgecomb, Cost Negotiator, Division of Cost Allocations, HEW Region IV.

Joseph Handzo, Director, Office of Cost Determination, Office of the Comptroller, U.S. Department of Labor.

Ben Gragg, Regional Cost Negotiator, U.S. Department of Labor, Region IV.

I extend special thanks to Mr. Gragg for his efforts in coordinating the comments from regional offices of the Office of Cost Determination and for his many suggestions on the initial drafts.

Additionally, I acknowledge the support I received from Charlie Tyer, Director of the University of South Carolina's Bureau of Governmental Research and Service, and from various University of South Carolina faculty and staff. Finally the assistance of three Bureau staff members is greatly appreciated—Bob Garey for helping edit the draft and Jane Lorick and Rose Douglas for typing the manuscript and correcting the punctuation and spelling.

Despite the wide review of this guide, the contents should not be interpreted as official federal policy. I assume full responsibility for the accuracy of the contents.

J.E.K.

Contents

CONTENTS

CONTENTS

1. Introduction to Indirect Cost Plans

The first section of this chapter introduces the subject of indirect cost allocation plans by explaining the terms and concepts involved in this accounting procedure. The second section describes the benefits that local governments can derive from preparing an indirect cost plan and applying the rates derived from the plan to federal grants.

THE JARGON OF INDIRECT COST PLANS

What are indirect costs? How do they relate to direct costs?

Direct costs for a federal grant program are those costs that clearly can be assigned to the program. For example, the salary and fringe benefits of a grant-funded position would be direct costs. *Indirect* or *overhead costs* cannot be attributed easily to a specific program providing services to the public. Indirect costs are usually incurred for "supportive" services that benefit various government programs. For example, the indirect costs of maintaining a courthouse or city hall that houses grant and locally funded programs cannot be readily assigned and charged to specific programs.

What indirect costs does the federal government allow local governments to charge to grants?

The major category of indirect costs chargeable to federal grants is operating costs of "central service agencies" that provide supportive services to other government agencies. These supportive services include personnel, administration, building and vehicle operation and maintenance, data processing, and accounting. Allowable indirect costs beyond central service agencies include the bonding of employees, insurance, audit services, and other central government costs that benefit all programs. Annual depreciation costs of usable buildings, motor vehicles, and other equipment not paid for through federal grants are also allowable as indirect costs.

What is an indirect cost allocation plan?

A cost allocation plan is a document that identifies allowable indirect costs of a governmental unit and distributes these costs to all government programs, including those funded through grants. For example, the cost allocation plan allocates a portion of the Finance Department's costs to the Public Works Department.

What costs are unallowable as indirect costs in the cost allocation plan?

The following types of costs are generally unallowable as indirect costs in cost allocation plans:

Capital expenditures on items such as equipment and buildings.

Salaries and expenses of council members.

Interest costs on borrowed funds.

Costs of "general government," including the tax collector and the mayor's office.

The category of "general government" is not clearly defined in the federal brochure (OASC–10*) and is very close to the definition of "central service agencies." In general, if the activities of central service agencies can be shown to benefit federal grant programs, their costs are allowable as indirect costs.

What is an indirect cost rate and how is it useful for federal programs?

As previously described, the nature of indirect costs —overhead—is that they cannot be assigned easily to specific departments or programs. The benefits provided by a chief executive, janitorial staff, or a purchasing officer are shared by various programs; and local governments generally do not charge all these supportive services to the programs. For most local government activities this is not a problem; council members and other citizens accept the fact that a portion of the budget is composed of "general government" functions not directly benefiting the public. However, for grant-reimbursable programs, the inability to assign overhead is a problem, because only

* U.S. Department of Health, Education, and Welfare, *Cost Principles and Procedures for Establishing Cost Allocation Plans and Indirect Cost Rates for Grants and Contracts with the Federal Government* (December 1976).

clearly justifiable expenses may be charged to grant programs. The alternative to charging supportive services directly to grants is to apply an "overhead" or "indirect cost" rate to grant expenditures. Such a rate reflects the relationship between a local government's overhead costs and its direct program costs; this relationship is assumed to apply also to grant programs operated by the jurisdiction. Although all program costs, including supplies, equipment, contractual services, and personnel, may be used as a basis for the rate, the federal guide (OASC–10) recommends the use of salaries only as the indirect cost base. The equation for the rate is the following:

$$\frac{\text{total indirect costs}}{\text{indirect cost base}} = \frac{\text{costs of central supportive services}}{\text{salary and wage costs of operating agencies}}$$

where operating agencies are all departments and offices not included as central support agencies.

BENEFITS OF INDIRECT COST PLANS

Who should prepare an indirect cost plan?

Cities, counties, school districts, and special purpose districts of all sizes should consider preparing indirect cost plans if they receive any federal grant funds at all. Also, states commonly require all their state agencies to prepare indirect cost plans for application to their federal grants. Even though a smaller jurisdiction may have much less to gain from the plan than a larger one, the smaller jurisdiction's plan will also generally be easier to complete. Local governments are not required to prepare a plan—only those wishing to recover indirect costs under grants. Preparation of a plan must precede indirect cost recovery.

What are the potential benefits of an indirect cost plan?

A local government can benefit financially from an indirect cost allocation plan in one or more of the following ways:

1.   Shift of Existing Grant Funds to Cover Indirect Costs. The most likely benefit from an indirect cost plan is to permit a unit to shift grant funds within its existing allocation to cover indirect costs. The example provided next illustrates the financial benefits to a jurisdiction from such a shift. A city with a $100,-000 federal grant award begins the year with the grant budget shown in the left column as follows:

6

	Initial Budget	Revised Budget
Salaries	$ 80,000	$ 70,000
Fringe benefits	12,000	10,000
Supplies	8,000	6,000
Indirect costs	0	14,000[a]
Total budget	$100,000	$100,000

[a] 20% indirect cost rate $\times$ $70,000 salaries.

After the city completes its indirect cost plan, the legislative body decides to request a shift of funds from the three budget categories to cover indirect costs, as shown in the right column. The $14,000 of indirect costs that the city's plan can justify is budgeted to cover existing general fund costs previously funded by the property tax and other general fund revenues. In other words, the budget is changed to reflect the federal government's bearing its share of the hidden, indirect costs of federal programs.

2. Additional Grant Revenue. Preparation of an indirect cost plan can also make it possible for a local government to receive additional grant funds to cover indirect costs. This is the best possible result of preparing a plan. Although a unit of government is not guaranteed additional funding after completion of an indirect cost plan, the plan can be offered as a justification for an increased grant allocation. A modification of the prior budget example is a city that receives an additional allocation to cover its indirect costs as shown here:

	Initial Budget	Revised Budget
Salaries	$ 80,000	$ 80,000
Fringe benefits	12,000	12,000
Supplies	8,000	8,000
Indirect costs	0	16,000[a]
Total	$100,000	$116,000

[a] $80,000 salaries × 20% indirect cost rate.

3. Use of Indirect Costs as Matching Funds for Grants. Indirect costs justified through an indirect cost plan may be used to satisfy cash matching requirements of federal grants (OASC–10, p. 23). Although this use of the indirect cost plan does not create additional revenues for the jurisdiction, the use of indirect costs to match federal funds may eliminate the need for additional local appropriations.

To what federal programs may indirect costs be applied?

Indirect costs may be charged to most federal grant programs as permitted in the federal regulations pertaining to each program. As defined in OASC–10, p. 32, a grant is "an agreement between the Federal Government and a local government whereby the Federal Government provides funds to carry out specified programs, services, or activities." This excludes General Revenue Sharing and Anti-Recession Fiscal Assistance. The most frequent application of indirect costs is to grants for operating programs as opposed to construction grants. However, indirect costs can be recovered under some construction grants. For construction grants, there may be a negotiated lump sum for overhead as permitted in OASC–10, p. 34.

What policy decisions regarding indirect costs must be made by the governing body of the jurisdiction?

No policy decision likely would be required in the second budget example just cited. The council would gladly accept the additional grant funds to cover the city's indirect costs. However, in the second example, the council faces the decision of possibly reducing direct services provided under the grant to allocate funds for indirect costs. In considering whether to shift funds from direct to indirect costs the council should be aware that the recovery of indirect costs through grants can help reduce the burden on local taxes to fund existing local services.

What factors determine the amount of reimbursements after local governments have completed indirect cost plans?

Although a local government cannot receive indirect cost reimbursements without a plan, preparation of a plan does not assure reimbursements. The amount of indirect costs that a jurisdiction may recover will depend on three major factors:

1. The Indirect Cost Rate Justified in the Plan. The overhead rate determined by the plan represents the maximum to be allowed for the jurisdiction.

2. Federal Laws and Regulations. The regulations for each federal grant establish a policy for reimbursing indirect costs. For example, the Comprehensive Employment and Training Act (CETA) regulations place a limit on the percentage of grant funds that may pay administrative costs and also restrict the types of indirect costs that a jurisdiction may charge to its CETA grant programs. Appendices 1 and 2 contain federal regulations from the CETA and Community Development Block Grant programs as examples of how indirect costs are treated in the regulations.

3. State Agency Policies. State agencies assigned

the responsibility of distributing federal funds may establish their own policies on passing through in-direct cost reimbursements to local governments. State agencies may not permit more reimbursement than allowed in the federal regulations, but they may permit less. Local officials should become aware of federal regulations pertaining to indirect costs allowed under their grant programs and also should obtain a written statement regarding indirect cost reimbursements to localities from each state agency that distributes federal funds to them. If local officials discover that the state agency policy differs from the federal regulations, they should determine who made the state policy and how the policy can be changed, if it is financially detrimental to local governments.

In summary, the purpose of indirect cost plans is to identify grant-reimbursable overhead costs and to provide an easy means for governmental units to permit the federal government to share in these costs. The regulations for preparing indirect cost plans are not intended to dictate grant funding levels to federal and state agencies. However, local officials should raise questions with appropriate policy-makers regarding any policy that appears to contradict the indirect cost plan concept—namely, that the federal government should share the cost of supportive services with local governments.

In what areas other than federal grants may indirect cost rates be applied?

Local governments may wish to apply indirect cost rates in the following areas outside of federal grants:

1. Fee Computations. Indirect cost rates may be used in computing fees for services provided by the jurisdiction to individual citizens, businesses, or other governmental units. For example, a per diem charge for housing another jurisdiction's prisoners in the county jail may have built into it an overhead rate. If a county's cost of housing a prisoner is $5.00 per day, a 20% overhead rate added to this would make the full-cost fee $6.00 per day. An indirect cost rate approved by an agency of the United States government is not legally enforceable between local governments, but an approved plan can help justify the use of an overhead rate.

2. Utility Operations. An indirect cost rate may be used to justify a local government's transferring revenues from its own utility operating fund to its general fund. For example, a city operating a water-sewer system may provide significant support services to that operation, including overall supervision, personnel management, and financial management, as well as building space. Through application of an indirect cost rate, the jurisdiction can justify the utility operation's reimbursing, in effect, the general fund for services provided through that fund. Such a practice forces users of the utility services, whether or not they are located in the jurisdiction, to share in the costs of the general government operations in proportion to their usage of the utility services.

3. Realistic Reflection of Overhead. Indirect cost rates may be used to demonstrate to local government managers and policy makers, as well as to citizens, the true costs of departmental operations. The rates help localities to reflect properly the overhead costs essential to any department's delivery of services.

The realistic reflection of overhead is a relatively new concern in governmental accounting. Business accountants are naturally concerned with overhead because these costs must enter into product and service pricing decisions. Before local and state government agencies were permitted to charge overhead to federal grants, the major application of indirect cost allocations to accounting by nonprofit organizations was by hospitals. The hospitals must justify the rates they charge to insurance companies, the federal government, and patients. Although allocation of overhead to government programs is relatively new, the basic reason for the allocation is the same for government agencies as for businesses: to assist in determining the total costs of providing specific goods and services to the customers.

2. Approval Process and Application of Approved Rates

Although most of this guide focuses on the plan preparation process, this chapter presents information to assist the preparer in understanding how the plan is approved and what he or she does with the plan and rates after approval.

PROCESS FOR APPROVAL OF INDIRECT COST PLANS

Who approves indirect cost plans for local governments?

Each local government needs only to seek approval of its plan by one federal agency, known as a "cognizant agency." The cognizant agency for a local government is generally the "Federal department which has the greatest dollar involvement" with the locality (OASC–10, p. 4). A selected number of large jurisdictions are assigned cognizant agencies in the Federal Guide OASC–9.* All other governmental units should "adopt" a cognizant agency with which they have the largest dollar involvement. Any question regarding a locality's cognizant agency should be directed to the following: Financial Management Branch, Budget Review Division of the United States Office of Management and Budget, Washington, D.C. 20503.

From which office of the cognizant agency should a locality seek approval of its plan?

Federal Guide OASC–10 assigns to the regional or national office of each federal agency the responsibility for approving cost allocation plans. As examples, the regional office of the Department of Housing and Urban Development usually is assigned the

* *A Reference for State and Local Governments of Federal Agencies' Responsibility for Audit and Approval of Cost Allocation Plans.* (This publication is out of print, but assignments may be determined by contacting the Office of Management and Budget.)

responsibility of approving plans, but the national office of the U.S. Environmental Protection Agency is assigned the approval authority. See Appendix 3 for the addresses of some of the offices to contact.

Is a jurisdiction required to obtain approval of its indirect cost plan from each federal agency providing funds to it?

One objective of the indirect cost plan approval process is to eliminate the need for governmental units to prepare more than one plan to satisfy different federal agencies. Therefore, the cognizant agency is assigned the responsibility of approving indirect cost plans on behalf of all other federal agencies (OASC–10, p. 3). Under the simplified method described in Chapter 4, the cognizant agency approves both the cost allocation plan and the single indirect cost rate. A federal agency, however, may question the rate approved by another federal agency and require the jurisdiction to compute a special rate for the program it funds. Under the multirate method described in chapters 5 and 6, the cognizant agency approves only the cost allocation plan and the indirect cost proposals for the programs that it helps to fund. Jurisdictions must seek approval of their indirect cost proposals for other departments from the federal agencies partially funding those local departments' programs.

What is involved in the approval process?

OASC–10, p. 7, states that "local government cost allocation plans need be submitted for approval only upon request of the cognizant federal agency or its authorized representative (in some instances state agencies act as representatives). Otherwise, localities need only retain the plans . . . and have them available for review by the Federal Government." The approval by the cognizant agency does not necessarily follow a detailed review of the locality's plan by that agency. For example, the southeastern regional office of one federal agency has a policy of requiring submission of plans, but of not reviewing the plans. The agency indicates to the jurisdiction that the office is aware ("cognizant") of the plan, but that the future auditors of the unit's grants will be responsible for determining the legitimacy of all grant charges—including indirect cost charges. Another cognizant agency in the southeast reviews plans and negotiates with localities before approving the rates. Local officials are encouraged to contact appropriate people in their cognizant agencies before completing their plans to determine the agencies' submission and review requirements.

When should a locality prepare its plan?

According to federal guidelines, indirect cost plans should be submitted within six months after the close of the locality's fiscal year. However, local officials should proceed to develop plans as soon as they are able to do so and then request an extension of the six-month limitation, if required, as permitted by OASC–10, p. 10. Plans must be updated annually.

How is the approval of indirect cost plans formalized?

To formalize the indirect cost plan and rate approval, the cognizant agency enters into a written agreement with the local government. The cognizant agency will determine the type of agreement it will approve. Appendix 4 contains example indirect cost rate agreements.

What types of agreements may be approved by a federal agency?

Three types of agreements are discussed in OASC–10, p. 15: provisional-final, predetermined, and fixed with carry-forward. The carry-forward method, the most common, involves the federal agency's approval of a fixed rate, based on the current year's budgeted costs or the previous year's actual costs. After the close of the fiscal year for which the plan was prepared, the actual indirect and direct costs are determined and an adjusted rate is computed. In preparing the annual revision of the indirect cost plan based on actual expenditures, the preparer is also computing the adjusted costs and rate.

The differences between actual costs and the previously computed costs are adjusted in a subsequent year's plan. Appendix 5 contains a table from OASC–10 illustrating the adjustment for a carry-forward agreement.

APPLICATION OF APPROVED INDIRECT COST RATES TO GRANTS

What is the next step after an indirect cost rate has been approved?

After a jurisdiction receives approval of its cost allocation plan and indirect cost rate(s), local officials should seek to include indirect costs in the budgets for the grants. For grants that have already been awarded, localities should request additional funding to cover indirect costs. If additional funding is unavailable, the locality should seek grant budget amendments to shift funds from direct cost categories to indirect costs, after the approval by the city or county council or other governing body. For grants that the locality is applying for, the indirect cost rate and accompanying costs should be included in the grant application's budget. Most grant budget forms include a separate line for indirect costs, as shown in tables 2.1 and 2.2 from the Office of Management and Budget's Circular A–102, *Uniform Administrative Requirements for Grants-in-Aid to State and Local Governments.*

How is the indirect cost rate applied to the grant budget to compute the budgeted indirect costs?

The approved indirect cost rate is multiplied by the budgeted salaries and wages to yield the amount of indirect costs. Indirect costs for a jurisdiction with a 20% rate would be computed as follows:

Grant Budget

Personnel	$50,000
Fringe benefits	7,500
Travel	1,000
Supplies	500
Total direct charges	$59,000
Indirect charges	$10,000 = \$50,000 \times 20\%$
Total budget	$69,000

Table 2.1 Application for Federal Assistance: Budget Data.

OMB Approval No. 80–R0186

PART III – BUDGET INFORMATION

SECTION A – BUDGET SUMMARY

Grant Program, Function or Activity (a)	Federal Catalog No. (b)	Estimated Unobligated Funds		New or Revised Budget		
		Federal (c)	Non-Federal (d)	Federal (e)	Non-Federal (f)	Total (g)
1.		$	$	$	$	$
2.						
3.						
4.						
5. TOTALS		$	$	$	$	$

SECTION B – BUDGET CATEGORIES

6. Object Class Categories	Grant Program, Function or Activity				Total
	(1)	(2)	(3)	(4)	(5)
a. Personnel	$	$	$	$	$
b. Fringe Benefits					
c. Travel					
d. Equipment					
e. Supplies					
f. Contractual					
g. Construction					
h. Other					
i. Total Direct Charges					
j. Indirect Charges					
k. TOTALS	$	$	$	$	$
7. Program Income	$	$	$	$	$

[a] Source: Office of Management and Budget (OMB) Circular A–102, *Uniform Administrative Requirements for Grants-in-Aid to State and Local Governments, 1977.*

Table 2.2 Application for Federal Assistance (Short-Form): Budget Data.

OMB Approval No. 80-R0185

APPLICATION FOR FEDERAL ASSISTANCE (Short Form)			
PART II – BUDGET DATA			
Object Class Categories	Current Approved Budget (a)	Change Requested (b)	New or Revised Budget (c)
1. Personnel			
2. Fringe Benefits			
3. Travel			
4. Equipment			
5. Supplies			
6. Contractual			
7. Construction			
8. Other			
9. Total Direct Charges			
10. Indirect Charges			
11. TOTAL			
12. Federal Share			
13. Non-Federal Share			
14. Program Income			

15. Detail on Indirect Costs:

Type of Rate (Mark one box)   ☐ Provisional   ☐ Predetermined

                          ☐ Final   ☐ Fixed

Rate _____ %   Base $ _____ Total Amount $ _____

PART III

Program Narrative Statement
(Attach additional sheets, if necessary)

ᵃ Source: OMB Circular A–102.

Table 2.3 Financial Status Report

FINANCIAL STATUS REPORT
(Follow instructions on the back)

1. FEDERAL AGENCY AND ORGANIZATIONAL ELEMENT TO WHICH REPORT IS SUBMITTED
2. FEDERAL GRANT OR OTHER IDENTIFYING NUMBER
OMB Approved No. 80-RO180
PAGE OF PAGES

3. RECIPIENT ORGANIZATION (Name and complete address, including ZIP code)

4. EMPLOYER IDENTIFICATION NUMBER
5. RECIPIENT ACCOUNT NUMBER OR IDENTIFYING NUMBER
6. FINAL REPORT ☐ YES ☐ NO
7. BASIS ☐ CASH ☐ ACCRUAL

8. PROJECT/GRANT PERIOD (See instructions)
FROM (Month, day, year) TO (Month, day, year)

9. PERIOD COVERED BY THIS REPORT
FROM (Month, day, year) TO (Month, day, year)

10.

STATUS OF FUNDS

PROGRAMS/FUNCTIONS/ACTIVITIES ►	(a)	(b)	(c)	(d)	(e)	(f)	TOTAL (g)
a. Net outlays previously reported	$	$	$	$	$	$	$
b. Total outlays this report period							
c. Less: Program income credits							
d. Net outlays this report period (Line b minus line c)							
e. Net outlays to date (Line a plus line d)							
f. Less: Non-Federal share of outlays							
g. Total Federal share of outlays (Line e minus line f)							
h. Total unliquidated obligations							
i. Less: Non-Federal share of unliquidated obligations shown on line h							
j. Federal share of unliquidated obligations							
k. Total Federal share of outlays and unliquidated obligations							
l. Total cumulative amount of Federal funds authorized							
m. Unobligated balance of Federal funds							

11. INDIRECT EXPENSE

a. TYPE OF RATE (Place "X" in appropriate box)				
☐ PROVISIONAL ☐ PREDETERMINED ☐ FINAL ☐ FIXED				
b. RATE	c. BASE	d. TOTAL AMOUNT	e. FEDERAL SHARE	

12. REMARKS: Attach any explanations deemed necessary or information required by Federal sponsoring agency in compliance with governing legislation.

13. CERTIFICATION
I certify to the best of my knowledge and belief that this report is correct and complete and that all outlays and unliquidated obligations are for the purposes set forth in the award documents.

SIGNATURE OF AUTHORIZED CERTIFYING OFFICIAL

TYPED OR PRINTED NAME AND TITLE

DATE REPORT SUBMITTED

TELEPHONE (Area code, number and extension)

260-101 EXHIBIT 1

STANDARD FORM 269 (7-76)
Prescribed by Office of Management and Budget
Circulars No. A-102 and A-110

a Source: OMB Circular A-102.

How is the reimbursement for indirect costs computed and requested?

Financial reporting of indirect costs and requests for reimbursements of indirect costs are made on the same forms as for direct costs. For example, the Federal Financial Status Report form shown as Table 2.3 includes a separate box, #11, for reporting indirect expenses for the period. The amount of indirect expenses for a reporting period is computed by multiplying the indirect cost rate by the grant salary expenses for the period. This computation is illustrated here for a grant with $10,000 in salaries for a quarter:

$10,000 Salary expenses for 1st quarter
× 0.20 Indirect cost rate
$ 2,000 Indirect charges made to grant for 1st quarter

3. Optional Methods of Preparing Indirect Cost Allocation Plans

Five alternative methods are available to governmental units for the preparation of indirect cost allocation plans, as described in OASC–10, pp. 47–69. These five variations may be summarized in the two basic categories described next:

Simplified Method and Long Form Method

1 Simplified Single-Rate Method. OASC–10, pp. 67–68, refers to this as the "Consolidated Local Central Service Cost Allocation Plan and Indirect Cost Proposal." This method, which may only be used by local and not state governments, assumes no differences in the levels of service provided by central service agencies to operating departments. The indirect costs for the entire local government are divided by the salary and wage costs for all the operating agencies to yield one average indirect cost rate for the jurisdiction. This rate may be applied to any grant program operated by any department.

2 Multirate Long Form Method. This second principal method encompasses the sample formats included on OASC–10, pp. 49–66. In contrast to the single-rate method, the long form takes into consideration the differing levels of centralized services provided to operating agencies. For example, it considers that the Parks and Recreation Department for a city occupies more building space than the Police Department and therefore benefits more than the Police Department from building maintenance services.

The long form method allocates or assigns the costs of supportive services to user agencies on some rational basis that relates dollars to levels of service. For example, the costs of a purchasing agent's services might be allocated among the departments on the basis of the relative number of purchase orders issued for each department. For each operating agency the costs allocated to it from each indirect cost area are totaled, and this figure is entered into the computation of a separate indirect cost rate for that department. The departmental rate would be applied to any grant program operated by that department.

How much work is required to prepare a plan using each of the methods?

It is only possible to provide order-of-magnitude estimates of time requirements for preparing plans using these methods, because the time required will depend on the preparer's familiarity with the federal guidelines and the quality of the locality's financial management system. A safe statement is that the long form method is exceedingly more difficult than the single-rate method. As an example, I spent over 100 hours preparing a long form plan for one city with significant assistance from city staff. The single-rate plan, on the other hand, required less than one day's effort for that city.

Which jurisdictions should consider using the short form method in preparing their plans?

Because of the advantages of the long form method already noted, larger jurisdictions should consider using it. However, for many small cities, counties, school districts, and special purpose districts, the simplified method may be adequate. An arbitrary guideline suggested here is that any local government with an operating budget below $10 million should consider using the short form method.

What are the advantages of preparing a long form plan over a single-rate plan?

Despite the large time investment required in preparing a plan using the long form method, the method can be advantageous to the larger jurisdictions because it yields significantly higher rates than the single-rate method. For example, one city's indirect cost rate computed by me using the single rate method is approximately 18%, while some of the departmental rates computed with the long form method range above 30%. The reason for the large differential is that the long form method permits jurisdictions to include indirect costs within operating departments in computing the indirect cost rates. For example, the supportive and administrative services provided by a police chief's office to a police department could be added to central service agencies' indirect costs in computation of the indirect cost rate. The amount of departmental indirect costs can be significant, and the long form plan is particularly advantageous to jurisdictions whose departments with high departmental and other indirect costs assigned to them also operate the grant programs.

May a jurisdiction prepare a plan using the single-rate method and later prepare a long form plan?

A local government may prepare the single-rate plan and update it with a long form plan when time permits, with the approval of the cognizant agency.

What should be considered in deciding between the two types of plans?

The large investment in preparing a long form plan—in taking existing staff off other projects or in paying someone else to prepare the plan—must be weighed against the potential financial benefits from the higher indirect cost rates that the long form plan will yield. The jurisdiction should examine federal regulations and state policies regarding limitations on indirect costs to determine whether the higher rates could be used. For example, a locality that computes a 15% rate using the single-rate method should determine whether a 25% or higher rate, which might result for a department under a long form plan, could be applied to any current or anticipated grants.

In summary, a jurisdiction should consider the following variables in deciding whether a long form plan would be useful:

1 Size of the jurisdiction.
2 Quality of the accounting system.
3 Dollar amount of federal grants.
4 Types of federal grants and applicability of indirect costs to them.
5 How close the jurisdiction is to any ceilings on allowable administrative costs.
6 Available staff time.

4. Procedures for Preparing Short Form Plan

This chapter describes in detail the procedures for preparing a single-rate cost allocation (short form) plan. (The following two chapters describe the long form method, and Chapter 7 discusses the contents of the final plan under both methods. Readers may omit chapters 5 and 6 if they choose the short form method.)

Two examples are included to aid the explanation: a county with a budget of $2 million and a city with a budget of nearly $6 million. These examples are adapted from the approved cost allocation plans of the jurisdictions.

USE OF INDIRECT COST RATE COMPUTATION FORM

Preparation of a simplified cost allocation plan requires completion of the form illustrated in Table 4.1, modeled after the example format found in OASC–10, p. 68. When completed, the form becomes the cost allocation plan, which yields the two components of the indirect cost rate equation at the bottom of the form—total indirect costs and direct salary and wage costs. The steps described in this chapter focus on the preparation of this form, which is shown in its various stages of completion.

Although OASC–10 does not require any tables in addition to the cost allocation plan itself, the preparation of some supplementary tables will aid staff in developing backup to explain the derivation of the figures in the plan. Throughout, supplementary tables are used where appropriate. Because these tables are optional, they may be submitted with the plan or referenced by footnotes in the plan and retained for possible audit. Preparers should observe the following rule: every number in the cost allocation plan should be traceable to the audit, budget, or backup working papers. Preparers should build backups as if they will not be available next year to explain the plans' preparation.

Table 4.1 Sample Format: Consolidated Central Service Cost Allocation Plan and Indirect Cost Proposal for Fiscal Year Ended June 30, 19——

Table 4.1
SAMPLE FORMAT
CONSOLIDATED CENTRAL SERVICE COST ALLOCATION PLAN
AND INDIRECT COST PROPOSAL
FOR FISCAL YEAR ENDED JUNE 30, 19__

					Direct Costs	
Indirect Cost Pool:	Total	Unallowable Costs	Indirect Costs	Salaries and Wages	All Other Costs
Total Indirect Cost Pool					
Indirect Cost Base:					

Total Indirect Cost Base

GRAND TOTAL

INDIRECT COST RATE COMPUTATION:

$$\frac{\text{Allowable Indirect Costs}}{\text{Direct Salary \& Wage Costs}} = \underline{\qquad} \%$$

Step 1. Decide on the Basis to Be Used for the Preparation of the Cost Allocation Plan

Budget or Financial Report

Localities are permitted to use their adopted budget or latest audited financial report as a basis for the preparation of the cost allocation plan and rates. The plan will therefore "reflect either a past period's cost experience or a projection of a future year's expected cost" (OASC–10, p. 14). In either case, the cost allocation plan represents an estimate of indirect costs incurred during a grant period.

Basis for First Plan and Succeeding Plans

Whether the budget or audit is used largely depends on the time of the fiscal year when the plan is being prepared and the requirements established by the cognizant agency. For example, a city considering which basis to use for its first plan might have the following schedule for completion of its budget and audit:

June 1, 1979:   Budget adopted fiscal 1979–
                       1980

July 1, 1979:	Beginning of 1979–1980 fiscal year
October 1, 1979:	Audited financial reports for fiscal year 1978–1979 completed
June 30, 1980:	End of 1979–1980 fiscal year

If this example city were considering to proceed in June 1979 with the preparation of a fiscal year 1980 plan, the budget should be used as a basis. After October 1, either basis could be used. In updating the plan for the second year, it will be preferable for the city to wait until October 1980 and use the audited figures for fiscal year 1979–80. The first year's plan, based either on the estimate (budget) of the current year's costs or a previous year's costs, will necessarily yield an estimate of the jurisdiction's direct and indirect costs. Therefore, the cognizant agency will require the second and succeeding years' plans to be based on actual expenditures for the years in which the indirect cost reimbursements were received.

Step 2. Identify and List the Indirect Costs Areas

After the preparer determines the basis for the plan, he lists the locality's indirect cost areas, known as "pools." Table 4.2 presents the major local government indirect costs pools, which fall into one of the following three major categories:

Three Major Indirect Cost Areas

1.   Central Service Agencies. As discussed in Chapter 1, central service agencies provide to other local government agencies supportive services such as general supervision, maintenance, repair, and financial management. The seven major central service agency functions listed in Table 4.2 may be provided by a

Table 4.2   Major Allowable Indirect Cost Areas for Local Governments[a]

Indirect Cost Areas[b]	Description
Central Service Agencies	
Building operation and maintenance (B17, C2)	Allowable indirect costs include utilities for buildings, janitorial services, and cleaning supplies
Central stores and warehouse (B8)	Costs of operating a central store or warehouse facility may be counted as indirect costs. Materials, supplies, and other costs charged to user agency budgets may not be included as indirect costs

Table 4.2 (Continued)

Indirect Cost Areas[b]	Description
Chief executive[c]	Salaries and other costs of the appointed chief executive's office are allowable. Costs of the mayor's office or legislative expenses are unallowable
City or county attorney (A16)	Costs of legal services of the chief legal officer of a jurisdication are allowable if he or she provides services to federal grant programs
Data processing (C1)	This cost area includes data processing services, as well as equipment rental costs. If users are charged for data processing, they should all be charged the same rate, and direct charges to users should not also be counted as indirect costs. See "Depreciation and Use Allowances," OASC–10, p. 17

Finance
  Accounting (B1)
  Budgeting (B6)
  Disbursing of
    funds (B12)
  Purchasing (B24)
	This area includes costs of a finance department, clerk-treasurer's office, or other agency providing the services listed to the left. The locality must be prepared to show that the office provides benefits to federal grant programs. Costs of audits "necessary for the administration and management of functions related to grant programs" (B4) are also allowable

Table 4.2 (Continued)

Indirect Cost Areas[b]	Description
Personnel administration and payroll preparation (B21 and B22)	Costs of centralized personnel administration activities, including the following are allowable: payroll preparation, employee records maintenance, recruitment, training, and classification
Vehicle maintenance/garage (B20)	Operating costs of a locality's central vehicle maintenance facility are allowable indirect costs. Parts, supplies, labor, and overhead are allowable as indirect costs as long as they are not charged to user agencies either directly or through vehicle rentals

Nondepartmental Cost Areas

Building rentals (C2)	The rental of building space for grant and other programs is allowable if the rent is not charged as a direct cost to the grant
Fringe benefits Central service agencies (B13)	Where the employer's share of fringe benefits for the locality's employees are charged to nondepartmental accounts, the prorata portion attributable to central service agencies may be counted as indirect costs. Fringe benefits of grant-

Table 4.2 (Continued)

Indirect Cost Areas[b]	Description
	funded employees should always be charged as direct costs to grants
Insurance and bonding (B5, C4)	Costs of premiums on bonds covering employees who handle public funds are allowable. Also, the cost of insurance on buildings, vehicles, and other equipment are allowable
Memberships (B19)	Under certain conditions (see OASC–10, p. 42), the costs of memberships in civic, business, technical, and professional organizations that benefit grant programs directly or indirectly are allowable. For example, a fee paid to a regional council might be included in this cost category
Printing or mailing operation (B23, B27)	The operating costs of a printing/duplicating and mail room are allowable if they are not charged to user agencies. For example, if the paper supplies for a photocopying operation are charged to users but not the labor and machine operating costs, the labor and machine costs may be counted as indirect costs. Postage may be included if it is not charged to user departments
Telephone and other communication (B9)	Costs of a centralized telephone system (for example, a Centrex system) are allowable as indirect costs if they

Table 4.2 (Continued)

Indirect Cost Areas[b]	Description
	are not charged to users of the system
Workmen's Compensation and Unemployment Insurance (B13)	Workmen's Compensation and Unemployment Insurance costs charged to a nondepartmental account are allowable as indirect costs, or they may be charged as direct costs to grants

Depreciation and Use Allowances

Building depreciation or use allowance (B11)	Depreciation on local government buildings not constructed or purchased by federal grant funds is allowable as an indirect cost. Straight-line depreciation may be used or 2% may be applied to the acquisition cost of buildings to yield an annual use allowance
Depreciation or use allowance on motor vehicles and other equipment (B11)	Depreciation on motor vehicles and other equipment owned by the locality and not purchased by federal grant funds is an allowable indirect cost. Alternatively, a use allowance of $6^2/_3\%$ may be applied to the acquisition cost of the vehicles or other equipment. The "other equip-

Table 4.2 (Continued)

Indirect Cost Areas[b]	Description
	ment" may include printing or data processing equipment, with the data processing equipment requiring the approval of the grantor agency (OASC–10, pp. 42–43)

[a] This is a list of only the major indirect cost areas noted in OASC–10, pp. 39–44. Some jurisdictions will find other indirect cost categories such as professional services, advertising, employee morale and welfare services, and advisory council costs that may be allowable. See Table 4.3 for a partial listing of unallowable cost areas.

[b] References shown in parentheses pertain to cost items in OASC–10's "Standards for Selected Items of Cost," pp. 39–44. Items with a "B" are categorized as "allowable" costs; items with a "C" are "allowable with approval of grantor agency."

[c] The city or county administrator-manager is not listed as a separate allowable cost area in OASC–10, but a city manager is included in the example, p. 68, as a central service agency.

few or many separate offices, depending on the size of the local government.

2. Nondepartmental. Certain charges to nondepartmental accounts are allowable as indirect costs if the functions generally benefit the locality's agencies.

3. Depreciation and Use Allowance. Although capital expenditures are not usually allowable as indirect costs, a prorated portion of the costs of buildings and equipment may be allowed as depreciation, or as a depreciation substitute known as a "use allowance."

Unallowable Cost Areas

Table 4.3, as a companion to Table 4.2, lists the major cost areas that are unallowable as indirect cost pools. The one vague unallowable indirect cost area

Table 4.3 Costs Unallowable as Indirect Costs to Federal Grants

Unallowable Cost Areas[a]	Description
Capital costs (C3)	Capital costs of such items as buildings, land, vehicles, and equipment should not be included in computing indirect costs. The only way that the cost of capital items (excluding land) should be included as indirect costs is on a depreciated or use allowance basis. See OASC–10, p. 40
Contingencies (D2)	Appropriations to contingency funds for unforeseen events are unallowable

Table 4.3 (Continued)

Unallowable Cost Areas[a]	Description
Donations/ contributions (D3)	Donations or contributions, including those to community organizations are unallowable
General government operations[b]	Expenses required to carry out "general government" functions are unallowable. Examples include the mayor's office, salaries of council members, and tax collection activities
Interest and other debt service (D7)	Interest on debt and other debt-related costs are unallowable
Legislative expenses (D6, 8)	Salaries of the governing body and the elected chief executive are unallowable[c]

[a] References shown in parentheses pertain to cost items in OASC–10's "Standards for Selected Items of Cost," p. 44.

[b] OASC–10, p. 1, does not clearly define "general government," and there is a fine line between general government and central service agencies.

[c] At this printing the Office of Management and Budget is considering a change to OMB Circular 74–4 (in OASC–10) that would permit travel expenses of chief executives and governing bodies if such travel is related to grant programs. *See Federal Register,* September 5, 1979, p. 51921.

included in OASC–10 is "general government operations." The intent of OASC–10 appears to be to
eliminate from the indirect cost pool those general
government functions that cannot clearly be shown
to provide direct benefits to federal grant programs.
Examples of general government functions include
tax assessment and collection, which could only be
justified very tenuously as benefiting grant programs.
Where the tax collection function is performed in a
finance office that provides functions allowable as
indirect cost pools, it may be necessary to separate
the office's budget into activities as described in Step
3, which follows.

Examples

Tables 4.4a and 4.4b display on the cost allocation
plan forms the indirect cost areas for the City and
County examples. In the City Example, the General
Services Department (line 4) is divided into its com-
ponent functions to match the general categories
listed in OASC–10. This breakdown is not always
necessary, but it does aid in justifying the inclusion of
the agencies in the indirect cost pool. In addition, the
breakdown permits the preparer to exclude any portion of an agency's operation that is not an allowable
indirect cost area.

Table 4.4a Identification of Indirect Cost Pool for City Example: Consolidated Central Service Cost Allocation Plan and Indirect Cost Proposal for Fiscal Year Ended June 30, 19——.

CITY EXAMPLE
CONSOLIDATED CENTRAL SERVICE COST ALLOCATION PLAN
AND INDIRECT COST PROPOSAL

FOR FISCAL YEAR ENDED JUNE 30, 19__

			Total	Unallowable Costs	Indirect Costs	Direct Costs	
		Indirect Cost Pool:				Salaries and Wages	All Other Costs
1	1	City Manager's Office					
2	2	Clerk-Treasurer's Office:					
3	3	Accounting and Payroll					
4	4	General Services Department:					
5	5	Garage					
6	6	Building Maintenance					
7	7	Personnel and Purchasing					
8	8	Computer Services					
9	9	Non-Departmental:					
10	10	Insurance and Bonding					
11	11	Memberships					
12	12	Postage and Photocopying					
13	13	Building Depreciation					
14	14	Vehicle Use Allowance					
15	15						
16	16	Total Indirect Cost Pool					
17	17						
18	18	Indirect Cost Base:					
19	19	Mayor and Council					
20	20	Planning & Community Dev.					
21	21	Police					
22	22	Fire					
23	23	Codes Enforcement					
24	24	Engineering					
25	25	Public Works					
26	26	Parks and Recreation					
27	27	Water - Sewer					
28	28	Genl. Svces. Dept.: Airport					
29	29	Clerk-Treasurer's Office:					
30	30	Tax Collection					
31	31	Non-Departmental: Other					
32	32	Debt Service					
33	33						
34	34	Total Indirect Cost Base					
35	35						
36	36	GRAND TOTAL					

Table 4.4b Identification of Indirect Cost Pool for County Example: Consolidated Central Service Cost Allocation Plan and Indirect Cost Proposal for Fiscal Year Ended June 30, 19——.

COUNTY EXAMPLE
CONSOLIDATED CENTRAL SERVICE COST ALLOCATION PLAN
AND INDIRECT COST PROPOSAL
FOR FISCAL YEAR ENDED JUNE 30, 19__

	Indirect Cost Pool:	Total	Unallowable Costs	Indirect Costs	Direct Costs Salaries and Wages	Costs All Other Costs
1	County Administrator's Office					
2	General Administration: Finance					
3	Purchasing, & Personnel					
4	Public Buildings Maintenance					
5	Garage					
6	Audit					
7	Non-Departmental					
8	Memberships					
9	Postage					
10	Bonding and Insurance					
11	Fringe Benefits of Central					
12	Service Agencies					
13	Buildings Use Allowance					
14						
15	Total Indirect Cost Pool					
16						
17	Indirect Cost Base:					
18	County Council					
19	Tax Assessor					
20	Detention Center					
21	Public Works					
22	Landfill and Rural Collection					
23	Clerk of Court, Other Judicial					
24	Tax Auditor					
25	Treasurer and Tax Collector					
26	Coroner					
27	Sheriff					
28	Election Commission and Voter					
29	Registration					
30	Social Services					
31	Ambulance Services					
32	Contributions					
33	Fringe Benefits of Operating					
34	Agencies					
35	Contingency & Debt Retirement					
36	Other Agencies					
37	Federal Grant Programs					
38						
39	Total Indirect Cost Base					
40						
41	GRAND TOTAL					

Step 3. Identify the Total Costs for Each Indirect Cost Pool

This step of identifying the indirect costs for each cost pool is the most time-consuming part of the process, mainly because the budget and audit for a locality usually do not present the indirect cost pools as self-contained accounting units. The identification of indirect costs must follow one guiding principle: indirect and direct costs must be handled consistently; if costs are charged to departments and grant programs as direct costs, then they should not be included in the cost allocation plan as indirect costs. The inclusion of costs in a grant as direct costs and the same costs in the allocation plan as indirect costs would constitute "double-dipping" by the jurisdiction. For example, if a locality charges a vehicle rental to its departments and grant programs to cover a portion of the vehicle maintenance and operation costs, then the costs covered by the rentals should not be included as indirect costs.

The costs identified in this step are entered in column 1 of the cost allocation plan as illustrated in Tables 4.5a and 4.5b for the City and County examples. Because indirect cost areas are not always clearly separated in the budget and audit and because of possible overlapping of direct and indirect costs, the preparer must evaluate each indirect cost

Table 4.5a City Example: Consolidated Central Service Cost Allocation Plan and Indirect Cost Proposal for Fiscal Year Ended June 30, 19——.

			1	2	3	4	5
						Direct Costs	
		Indirect Cost Pool:	Total	Unallowable Costs	Indirect Costs	Salaries and Wages	All Other Costs
1	1	City Manager's Office	$ 45540	—	$ 45540		
2	2	Clerk-Treasurer's Office:					
3	3	Accounting and Payroll	73360	$ 1000	72360		
4	4	General Services Department:					
5	5	Garage	134120	20000	114120		
6	6	Building Maintenance	49500	500	49000		
7	7	Personnel and Purchasing	14650	—	14650		
8	8	Computer Services	26900	—	26900		
9	9	Non-Departmental:					
10	10	Insurance and Bonding	27000	—	27000		
11	11	Memberships	18800		18800		
12	12	Postage and Photocopying	9500		9500		
13	13	Building Depreciation	24000	—	24000		
14	14	Vehicle Use Allowance	44210	—	44210		
15	15						
16	16	Total Indirect Cost Pool	$ 467580	$ 21500	446080		
17	17						

CITY EXAMPLE — CONSOLIDATED CENTRAL SERVICE COST ALLOCATION PLAN AND INDIRECT COST PROPOSAL — FOR FISCAL YEAR ENDED JUNE 30, 19__

4912 - Buff / 8912 - Green / 4212 - White

pool separately to assure consistency and accuracy. The following are six indirect cost areas illustrating some of the considerations the preparer will face.

Case A. Indirect Cost Pool Is a Separate Accounting Entity

This is the simplest situation in which an entire budget unit comprises an allowable indirect cost area. The following are examples of this case:

Table 4.5b County Example: Consolidated Central Service Cost Allocation Plan and Indirect Cost Proposal for Fiscal Year Ended June 30, 19——.

COUNTY EXAMPLE
CONSOLIDATED CENTRAL SERVICE COST ALLOCATION PLAN
AND INDIRECT COST PROPOSAL
FOR FISCAL YEAR ENDED JUNE 30, 19__

			1	2	3	4	5
						Direct	Costs
				Unallowable	Indirect	Salaries	All Other
		Indirect Cost Pool:	Total	Costs	Costs	and Wages	Costs
1	1	County Administrator's Office	$ 29350	—	$ 29350		
2	2	General Administration: Finance					
3	3	Purchasing, & Personnel	24300	—	24300		
4	4	Public Buildings Maintenance	54400	$ 9800	44600		
5	5	Garage	75700	15100	60600		
6	6	Audit	12000	—	12000		
7	7	Non-Departmental					
8	8	Memberships	11250	—	11250		
9	9	Postage	5800	—	5800		
10	10	Bonding and Insurance	1000	—	1000		
11	11	Fringe Benefits of Central					
12	12	Service Agencies	12030	—	12030		
13	13	Buildings Use Allowance	12000		12000		
14	14						
15	15	Total Indirect Cost Pool	$237830	$ 24900	$212930		
16	16						

City Example—Table 4.5a
    City Manager's Office (line 1)
    Computer Services Division (line 8).

County Example—Table 4.5b
    County Administrator's Office (line 1)
    Public Buildings Department (line 4)
    Garage (line 5).

Case B. Allowable Indirect Cost Pools Are Located in a Department with Nonallowable Areas

In this case, a basically central service department includes functions that are not supportive services. In the City Example, the General Services Department (Table 4.5a, line 4) includes the central services of vehicle operation and maintenance, building operation and maintenance, personnel, and purchasing. It also includes the city airport operation. A variation of this case is an operating agency providing central service functions—for example, a public works department that operates a vehicle maintenance facility.

Table 4.6 illustrates one method for separating the central service costs from the other costs of the department, using the City's General Services Department as an example. The method involves preparing a program, or activity budget for the department, if the functions are not already separated. All the objects of expenditure categories should first be listed, and the total costs identified in column 1. Next, the costs in column 1 should be distributed among the activities of the department. Table 4.6 illustrates a simplified version of this procedure in which only the major object code series are listed. It may be necessary to prepare this chart in more detail by listing the costs of individual object codes and individual positions.

Table 4.6 City Example: Activity Budget for General Services Department

Description	1 Total	2 Garage	3 Building Maintenance	4 Personnel and Purchasing	5 Airport
Personal services	$109,000	$ 65,000	$ 20,500	$ 11,500	$ 12,000
Fringe benefits	22,200	14,000	3,500	2,300	2,400
Contractual services	37,970	6,120	18,000	250	13,600
Materials and supplies	40,600	29,000	7,000	600	4,000
Equipment	20,500	20,000	500	—	—
Total	$230,270	$134,120	$ 49,500	$ 14,650	$ 32,000
			Indirect cost pool		Indirect cost base

Another example of a use for this methodology is the City's Clerk-Treasurer's Office (Table 4.5a, line 2). This office performs the central service functions of accounting and payroll, as well as the function of tax collection, which is not acceptable as an indirect cost pool. In a situation where one person performs both supportive services and other functions, the preparer may consider two options. He might split the employee's salary between the functions, based on timesheets kept by the individual for a long enough period of time to indicate a realistic distribution. Alternatively, the preparer might allocate all the individual's salary to the central service function and include a footnote explaining the allocation. The cognizant agency then has the option of allowing or disallowing a portion of the costs.

All functions separated from the indirect cost pool should be included at the bottom of the cost allocation plan as part of the indirect cost base as described in Step 6, presented later.

Case C. Nondepartmental Indirect Cost Pools

For most localities, a nondepartmental budget unit contains costs both allowable and unallowable as indirect costs. The same type of allocation suggested for Case B may be used for nondepartmental costs as illustrated in Tables 4.7a and 4.7b.

Table 4.7a City Example: Allocation of Nondepartmental Costs

Budget Acct. #	Description	Total	Allowable Indirect Costs	Other Costs
4016–610	Insurance	$ 10,000	$10,000	
4016–620	Contributions	20,000		$20,000
4016–630	Legal Services	10,200		10,200
4016–635	Bonding	17,000	17,000	
4016–638	Memberships	23,800	18,800	5,000
4016–640	Postage	12,200	7,200	5,000
4016–650	Photocopying	2,300	2,300	
4016–680	Equipment	50,000		50,000
	Total	$145,500	$55,300	$90,200
			Indirect cost pool	Indirect cost base

Where few cost areas occur in the nondepartmental budget unit, preparation of a chart might be unnecessary if proper footnotes are provided to explain all the cost areas.

**Table 4.7b County Example: Allocation of
Nondepartmental Costs**

Budget Acct. #	Description	Total	Allowable Indirect Costs	Other Costs
292–10	Printing	$ 5,000	$ 5,000	
292–11	Postage	4,500	4,500	
292–14	Memberships	18,800	18,800	
292–20	Legal services	20,000		$ 20,000
292–28	Insurance and bonding	27,000	27,000	
292–82	Contributions	20,200		20,200
292–89	Contingency	50,000		50,000
	Total	$145,500	$ 55,300	$ 90,200
			Indirect cost pool	Indirect cost base

Case D. Certain Costs of the Central Service Agency Are Charged to User Departments

The costs of a central service agency's operation that are charged directly to departments should be excluded from the indirect cost pool. For example, in Table 4.5b the County Example's Garage charges major parts and gasoline directly to user agencies.

These costs are not included in the $75,700 of indirect costs shown, line 5.

Case E. Fringe Benefits Are Charged to Nondepartmental Accounts

For a locality that charges the employer's share of employee fringe benefits to nondepartmental accounts, a separate schedule should be prepared. This schedule allocates a portion of the fringe benefits to employees of central service agencies. Table 4.8 illustrates one possible method for the allocation:

1 Identify the nondepartmental fringe benefit costs to be allocated.
2 Determine the total central service agency salaries and the salaries for all operating agencies.
3 Compute the percentage of the total salaries in the central service agencies combined and in the operating agencies combined.
4 Apply the percentages to the total nondepartmental fringes to determine the amount allowable as indirect costs.

The $12,030 resulting from this allocation is in-

Table 4.8 County Example: Allocation of Fringe Benefit Costs[a]

Fringe Benefit Costs to Be Allocated

Budget Account Number	Description	Costs to Be Allocated
130–120	Employees' insurance	$ 28,000
130–121	Social Security	38,500
130–122	State retirement	50,490
130–124	Workmen's Compensation	6,500
	Total	$123,490

Allocation of Fringe Benefit Costs

Agency	Total Salaries	Total Percent	Fringe Benefit Allocation	
Central service agencies	$ 92,217	9.74	$ 12,030	To indirect cost pool
Operating agencies	854,570	90.26	111,460	To indirect cost base
Total	$946,787	100.00	$123,490	

[a] Fringe benefits are charged to nondepartmental budget unit #130 for all county agencies. The allocation of fringe benefits between central service agencies and operating agencies is based on the total salaries for central service agencies in relation to the operating agencies' salaries.

cluded in the indirect cost pool (Table 4.5b line 12) and the balance in the indirect cost base.

Case F. Depreciation or Use Allowance on Buildings and Equipment

Depreciation cost is a portion of the original cost of a fixed asset that is considered an expense for a current period, such as one year. The inclusion of depreciation or a substitute for it as an indirect cost pool is allowed by OASC–10, pp. 40–41, but is not required. If a locality is preparing its first cost allocation plan, it might be advisable to omit depreciation for the first year unless the required figures are readily available. However, a local government with a good record of its fixed assets should include depreciation as an indirect cost.

The two classes of assets most commonly included in the cost allocation plan are motor vehicles and buildings. Under the consolidated method only vehicles assigned to central service agencies should be included in the computation, although all local government vehicles may be included in the long form plan. In considering which buildings to depreciate and include in the indirect cost pool, the preparer should at least include the major central office building for the local government—the city hall or county courthouse, for example. OASC–10 provides no guidance about whether depreciation on special purpose buildings such as recreation centers and fire stations should be included as indirect costs. This guide's recommendation is that only depreciation on special purpose buildings used by central service agencies (for example, the garage), or operating agencies receiving federal grants, should be included in the indirect cost pool. See Chapter 5, Step 7 for a more detailed discussion of depreciation.

Step 4. Exclude Unallowable Costs from the Indirect Cost Pool, and Total the Allowable Indirect Costs

In Step 3, the preparer enters all budgeted costs for the allowable indirect cost areas. Step 4 is the identification of the following unallowable costs within these budgets:

Unallowable Costs

- Federally Funded Costs. These are the portions of indirect costs pools that are already reimbursed as direct costs on grants. For example, one local government's director of finance keeps a record of the time he spends on a federal grant, and a portion of this person's salary and fringe benefits is treated as a direct charge to the grant.

- Capital Costs. All equipment items budgeted for the central service agencies should be excluded.

As shown in Tables 4.5a and 4.5b, these unallowable costs are identified in column 2 and subtracted from column 1; the difference is entered in column 3, which contains only allowable indirect costs. After this deduction, the allowable indirect costs are totaled, and one-half of the indirect cost rate formula is complete.

Step 5. List the Components of the Indirect Cost Base*

In steps 2, 3, and 4, the upper portion of the cost allocation plan—the indirect cost pool—is constructed; in steps 5 and 6, the indirect cost base is

* OASC–10, p. 68, uses the term "indirect cost base" to mean all cost areas not included in the indirect cost pool. Direct costs actually compose the indirect cost base.

Table 4.9a City Example: Identification of Indirect Cost Base.

CITY EXAMPLE
CONSOLIDATED CENTRAL SERVICE COST ALLOCATION PLAN
AND INDIRECT COST PROPOSAL
FOR FISCAL YEAR ENDED JUNE 30, 19__

17	17	
18	18	Indirect Cost Base:
19	19	Mayor and Council
20	20	Planning & Community Dev.
21	21	Police
22	22	Fire
23	23	Codes Enforcement
24	24	Engineering
25	25	Public Works
26	26	Parks and Recreation
27	27	Water - Sewer
28	28	Genl. Svces. Dept.: Airport
29	29	Clerk-Treasurer's Office:
30	30	Tax Collection
31	31	Non-Departmental: Other
32	32	Debt Service
33	33	

constructed. Step 5 lists functions to be considered for the base. As defined previously, the indirect cost base, which comprises the divisor of the indirect cost rate equation, equals the direct salary and wage costs for operating agencies benefiting from the indirect cost pool. In summary, all of a locality's budgeted or actual costs not part of the indirect cost pool should be included in column 1 under "indirect cost base." The following cost centers should be included:

Table 4.9b County Example: Identification of Indirect Cost Base.

		COUNTY EXAMPLE CONSOLIDATED CENTRAL SERVICE COST ALLOCATION PLAN AND INDIRECT COST PROPOSAL FOR FISCAL YEAR ENDED JUNE 30, 19__
17	17	Indirect Cost Base:
18	18	County Council
19	19	Tax Assessor
20	20	Detention Center
21	21	Public Works
22	22	Landfill and Rural Collection
23	23	Clerk of Court, Other Judicial
24	24	Tax Auditor
25	25	Treasurer and Tax Collector
26	26	Coroner
27	27	Sheriff
28	28	Election Commission and Voter
29	29	Registration
30	30	Social Services
31	31	Ambulance Services
32	32	Contributions
33	33	Fringe Benefits of Operating
34	34	Agencies
35	35	Contingency & Debt Retirement
36	36	Other Agencies
37	37	Federal Grant Programs

A. General Fund Operating Agencies

All general fund operating agencies should be listed as illustrated in lines 19 through 26 of the City Example in Table 4.9a and lines 18 through 37 in the County Example in Table 4.9b. The large number of agencies that some localities have might cause a listing problem. It therefore might be preferable to consolidate agencies into broad functional areas as illustrated by the following groupings used by one county in its plan:

- Legislative and Administrative.

- Financial Administration.

- Judicial.

- Public Works.

- Public Safety.

- Social Services.

- Planning and Development.

- Conservation.

- Other.

B. Enterprise/Utility Fund Agencies

Water-sewer or other enterprise/utility operations operated by the local government should be included.

C. Sections of Central Service Agencies and Nondepartmental Units

The segments of mainly central service agencies that are not allowable indirect cost areas should be included in the indirect cost base. For example, the section of the City's Clerk-Treasurer's Office performing tax collection and the airport operation of the General Services Department are listed in Table 4.9a (lines 28 and 29) as part of the indirect cost base. In addition, other nondepartmental areas not allowable as indirect costs should be listed in the indirect cost base column.

D. Federal Grant Programs

Any federal grant program not included within published departmental budgets and not otherwise listed in the indirect cost base should also be included in the base. These programs may be included on one line, as in the County Example (Table 4.9b, line 37), or listed separately. It is important that all grant programs with personnel be included in the base if those grant programs benefit from the indirect cost functions. In other words, any grant program to which the indirect cost rate may be applied should be included in the base.

E. Debt Service, Capital, and Other Areas

The preparer should be able to reconcile the grand total of the cost allocation plan to some total in the financial report or budget. To aid this reconciliation, he should include in the plan such items as debt service and general fund capital, even though the items do not include salary costs.

Step 6. Identify the Costs of Each Element of the Indirect Cost Base

This step is the identification of all costs of the indirect cost base areas in column 1 and the division of those costs between the three columns described next. Tables 4.10a and 4.10b show the cost listings for the two examples.

Column 2: Unallowable Costs

The identification of "unallowable costs" in column 2 is meaningless for the indirect cost base, since the

66

Table 4.10a City Example: Completed Cost Allocation Plan Form.

CITY EXAMPLE
CONSOLIDATED CENTRAL SERVICE COST ALLOCATION PLAN
AND INDIRECT COST PROPOSAL

FOR FISCAL YEAR ENDED JUNE 30, 19___

		Indirect Cost Pool:	Total	Unallowable Costs	Indirect Costs	Direct Costs Salaries and Wages	Direct Costs All Other Costs
1	1	City Manager's Office	$ 45540	–	$ 45540		
2	2	Clerk-Treasurer's Office:					
3	3	Accounting and Payroll	73360	$ 1000	72360		
4	4	General Services Department:					
5	5	Garage	134120	20000	114120		
6	6	Building Maintenance	49500	500	49000		
7	7	Personnel and Purchasing	14650	–	14650		
8	8	Computer Services	26900	–	26900		
9	9	Non-Departmental:					
10	10	Insurance and Bonding	27000	–	27000		
11	11	Memberships	18800	–	18800		
12	12	Postage and Photocopying	9500	–	9500		
13	13	Building Depreciation	24000	–	24000		
14	14	Vehicle Use Allowance	44210	–	44210		
15	15						
16	16	Total Indirect Cost Pool	$467580	$ 21500	$446080		
17	17						
18	18	Indirect Cost Base:					
19	19	Mayor and Council	$ 12600	–		$ 12600	
20	20	Planning & Community Dev.	110000	–		76350	$ 33650
21	21	Police	995000	$ 2000		705000	288000
22	22	Fire	804000	8000		609000	187000
23	23	Codes Enforcement	62000	–		48000	14000
24	24	Engineering	67000	–		46000	21000
25	25	Public Works	846000	43000		380000	423000
26	26	Parks and Recreation	499000	12000		321000	166000
27	27	Water - Sewer	1316000	18000		426000	872000
28	28	Genl. Svces. Dept.: Airport	32000	–		12000	20000
29	29	Clerk-Treasurer's Office:					
30	30	Tax Collection	15700	–		15700	–
31	31	Non-Departmental: Other	90200	50000		–	40200
32	32	Debt Service	570000	570000		–	–
33	33						
34	34	Total Indirect Cost Base	$5419500	$703000		$2651650	$2064850
35	35						
36	36	GRAND TOTAL	$5887080	$724500	$446080	$2651650	$2064850
37	37						

INDIRECT COST RATE COMPUTATION:

$$\frac{\text{Allowable Indirect Costs}}{\text{Direct Salary \& Wage Costs}} = \frac{\$446,080}{\$2,651,650} = 16.82\%$$

Table 4.10b County Example: Completed Cost Allocation Plan Form.

COUNTY EXAMPLE
CONSOLIDATED CENTRAL SERVICE COST ALLOCATION PLAN
AND INDIRECT COST PROPOSAL
FOR FISCAL YEAR ENDED JUNE 30, 19__

			1	2	3	Direct Costs 4	5
				Unallowable	Indirect	Salaries	All Other
		Indirect Cost Pool:	Total	Costs	Costs	and Wages	Costs
1	1	County Administrator's Office	$ 29350	—	$ 29350		
2	2	General Administration: Finance					
3	3	Purchasing, & Personnel	24300	—	24300		
4	4	Public Buildings Maintenance	54400	$ 9800	44600		
5	5	Garage	75700	15100	60600		
6	6	Audit	12000	—	12000		
7	7	Non-Departmental					
8	8	Memberships	11250	—	11250		
9	9	Postage	5800		5800		
10	10	Bonding and Insurance	1000	—	1000		
11	11	Fringe Benefits of Central					
12	12	Service Agencies	12030	—	12030		
13	13	Buildings Use Allowance	12000	—	12000		
14	14						
15	15	Total Indirect Cost Pool	$237830	$ 24900	$212930		
16	16						
17	17	Indirect Cost Base:					
18	18	County Council	$ 26800	—		$ 20500	$ 6300
19	19	Tax Assessor	83000	$ 4500		73300	5200
20	20	Detention Center	181180	4320		71400	105460
21	21	Public Works	301100	29000		122560	149540
22	22	Landfill and Rural Collection	103940	6000		38760	59180
23	23	Clerk of Court, Other Judicial	135190	900		88300	45990
24	24	Tax Auditor	23170			13130	10040
25	25	Treasurer and Tax Collector	31360	1050		28300	2010
26	26	Coroner	6830	250		4310	2270
27	27	Sheriff	226710	15440		148810	62460
28	28	Election Commission and Voter					
29	29	Registration	10740	900		8600	1240
30	30	Social Services	10710	—		—	10710
31	31	Ambulance Services	58890	6510		42500	9880
32	32	Contributions	173720	—		—	173720
33	33	Fringe Benefits of Operating					
34	34	Agencies	111460	—		—	111460
35	35	Contingency & Debt Retirement	65450	65450		—	—
36	36	Other Agencies	67300	—		59100	8200
37	37	Federal Grant Programs	196000	—		135000	61000
38	38						
39	39	Total Indirect Cost Base	$1813550	$134320		$854570	$824660
40	40						
41	41	GRAND TOTAL	$2051380	$159220	$212930	$854570	$824660
42							
43							

INDIRECT COST RATE COMPUTATION:

$$\frac{\text{Allowable Indirect Costs}}{\text{Direct Salary \& Wage Costs}} = \frac{\$212,930}{\$854,570} = 24.92\%$$

only important distinction for the base is between salary and nonsalary costs. However, OASC–10, p. 68, includes the column for the base for the sake of consistency. This column should contain for each line the following cost areas:

- Capital costs, including equipment, land, and buildings.

- Debt costs, including principal, interest, and other debt costs.

- Contingency fund costs.

Nonconstruction federal funds are not included in this column, because the salary costs are included in column 4. Alternatively, all unallowable costs for the base may be included in column 5, with "all other costs," since the column does not affect the indirect cost rate.

Column 3: Indirect Costs

This column is blank for all indirect cost base areas.

Column 4: Salary and Wage Costs

Entered in this column are salary and wage costs for all agencies that benefit from the indirect cost pool functions. Only salaries and wages are listed in this column; fringe benefits are not included. It is possible that an agency listed as part of the indirect cost base does not generally benefit from the services of the indirect cost areas. If the preparer can clearly show that the agency does not benefit, then the salaries of the agency may be excluded from the salary base and included in the "all other costs" column. Such a justification for exclusion of the salaries from the base should be stated in writing, possibly as a footnote to the plan. The total of column 4 provides the other half—the divisor—of the indirect cost rate formula.

Column 5: All Other Costs

All costs not entered in column 2 or 3 should be included in column 5. The sum of columns 2, 4, and 5 should equal column 1. After all the costs for each line in the base are entered in the appropriate columns, the indirect cost base columns are totaled. The grand total for each column is derived as follows:

Column 1.
    Indirect cost pool and indirect cost base.
Column 2.
    Indirect cost pool and indirect cost base.

Column 3.
   Indirect cost pool only.
Column 4.
   Indirect cost base only.
Column 5.
   Indirect cost base only.

Reconciliation of Totals

The grand total should be verified internally by making sure columns 2 through 5 equal column 1. The grand total should also be reconciled to the figures in the budget or financial report. In performing the reconciliation, the preparer should consider any use allowance or depreciation costs that would not appear in the budget or audit, as well as any grant funds added to the indirect cost base. It is recommended that the reconciliation be included in writing with the plan either as a footnote or separate schedule. The reconciliation for the County Example is the following:

Adopted fiscal 1979 budget total	$1,843,380
Plus building use allowance	12,000
Plus federal grant programs	196,000
Equals cost allocation plan grand total	$2,051,380

Table 4.11 Final Plan for City Example: Consolidated Central Service Cost Allocation Plan and Indirect Cost Proposal for Fiscal Year Ended June 30, 19___

	Total	Unallowable Costs	Indirect Costs	Direct Costs Salaries and wages	Direct Costs All Other Costs
Indirect Cost Pool					
City manager's office	$ 45,540	—	$ 45,540		
Clerk-treasurer's office:					
Accounting and payroll[a]	73,360	$ 1,000	72,360		
General services department[b]					
Garage	134,120	20,000	114,120		
Building maintenance	49,500	500	49,000		
Personnel and purchasing	14,650	—	14,650		
Computer services	26,900	—	26,900		
Nondepartmental[c]					
Insurance and bonding	27,000	—	27,000		
Memberships	18,800	—	18,800		
Postage and photocopying	9,500	—	9,500		
Building depreciation[d]	24,000	—	24,000		
Vehicle use allowance[e]	44,210	—	44,210		
Total indirect cost pool	$ 467,580	$ 21,500	$446,080		
Indirect Cost Base					
Mayor and council	$ 12,600	—		76,350	$ 33,650
Planning and community development	110,000	—		$ 12,600	—

72

Police	995,000	$ 2,000	705,000	288,000
Fire	804,000	8,000	609,000	187,000
Codes enforcement	62,000	—	48,000	14,000
Engineering	67,000	—	46,000	21,000
Public works	846,000	43,000	380,000	423,000
Parks and recreation	499,000	12,000	321,000	166,000
Water-sewer	1,316,000	18,000	426,000	872,000
General services department:				
Airport[b]	32,000	—	12,000	20,000
Clerk-treasurer's office:				
Tax collection[a]	15,700	—	15,700	—
Nondepartmental: Other[c]	90,200	50,000	—	40,200
Debt service	570,000	570,000	—	—
Total indirect cost base	$5,419,500	$703,000	$2,651,650	$2,064,850
Grand total	$5,887,080	$724,500 $446,080	$2,651,650	$2,064,850

Indirect cost rate computation:

$$\frac{\text{allowable indirect costs}}{\text{direct salary and wage costs}} = \frac{\$446,080}{\$2,651,650} = 16.82\%$$

[a] The costs of the Clerk-Treasurer's Office are allocated between the allowable indirect cost areas of accounting and payroll preparation and the unallowable area of tax collection.

[b] The General Service Department costs are allocated among three indirect cost pool areas and one unallowable indirect cost area, the Airport, included in the indirect cost base.

[c] Nondepartmental costs in the indirect cost base include legal services, contributions, and the contingency fund.

[d] Depreciation on City Hall computed by the straight-line method is included in the indirect cost pool.

[e] A 62/3% use allowance is multiplied by the original cost of the automotive equipment to compute the use allowance costs.

Step 7. Compute the Indirect Cost Rate

This step is the division of the indirect costs from column 3 by the salary and wage costs from column 4, illustrated with these two examples from Tables 4.13 and 4.14:

City Example

$$\frac{\text{indirect costs}}{\text{direct salary and wage costs}} = \frac{\$\ 446{,}080}{\$2{,}651{,}650} = 16.82\%$$

County Example

$$\frac{\text{indirect costs}}{\text{direct salary and wage costs}} = \frac{\$212{,}930}{\$854{,}570} = 24.92\%$$

Step 8. Prepare the Plan for Submission

The final step involves the tasks of getting the plan typed, adding footnotes, and preparing the attachments to the plan discussed in Chapter 7. Footnotes should be included to aid any person outside the agency in tracing figures in the plan to the budget, financial report, or working papers. If the preparer has completed tables and schedules supplementary to the plan (Tables 4.6, 4.7, 4.8), he should determine from the cognizant agency's contact person whether these should be submitted with the plan or retained by the locality. A final plan for the City Example is contained in Table 4.11.

5. The Long Form Cost Allocation Plan

As discussed in Chapter 3, the long form method of plan preparation takes into consideration the different levels of centralized services provided to operating agencies as opposed to the simplified method, which assumes equal services and the same indirect cost rate for the entire local government. The long form method results in two basic products:

1 The Central Service Cost Allocation Plan. This is a summary of all central service agency (indirect) costs allocated to the operating agencies. The example contained in Table 5.1 lists the operating agencies down the left side and the central service agencies across the top. The total indirect cost allocated to operating agencies is $4.1 million. Column A–1 for "fiscal analysis," for example, contains $457,739 ("subtotal"), which was allocated to the operating agencies of the local government. When the indirect costs allocated to each operating agency are added across, the total in the far right column is used to help compute the indirect cost rate for each agency. This chapter discusses the preparation of this table.

2 The Indirect Cost Rate Proposal. This second major product, illustrated as Table 5.2, includes the computation of the indirect cost rate of the bottom of the page. The allowable indirect costs in the far right column include $310,129.31 from the cost allocation plan (See "transportation," under "Operating Department Schedule" in Table 5.1) and $105,-705 of indirect costs within this department. Chapter 6 explains the preparation of the indirect cost rate proposal.

As previously discussed the long form method described in this chapter is much more difficult to prepare than the single-rate method outlined in Chapter 4. However, the rates resulting from the long form plan generally will be higher than from the short form rate. The reason for the difference is that local-

Operating Department Schedule	Fiscal Analysis A-1	Data Analysis and Processing B-1	County Board C-1	County Manager D-1	Personnel Department E-1
General Fund					CENTRAL SERVICE
Extension service	$ 961.25	$ 0	$ 464.15	$ 1,303.99	$ 4,764.62
County attorney	1,785.18	0	464.15	1,303.99	4,764.62
Circuit court	1,922.50	0	178.52	501.53	1,832.55
District court	6,362.58	294.18	1,273.44	3,577.61	13,072.16
Juvenile court	10,024.49	0	3,296.67	9,261.67	33,841.01
Court clerks	2,380.24	0	119.01	334.36	1,221.70
Commonwealth attorney	2,609.11	0	690.28	1,939.26	7,085.84
Sheriff and jail	14,235.69	294.18	3,986.95	11,200.93	40,926.86
Commissioner of revenue	9,429.43	21,377.31	3,058.64	8,592.95	31,397.62
Real estate assessments	3,799.24	18,795.03	868.80	2,440.80	8,918.39
Treasurer	8,971.69	41,839.38	2,606.39	7,322.40	26,755.17
Electoral board	1,510.54	2,974.52	226.12	635.28	2,321.22
Consumer affairs	1,190.12	0	404.64	1,136.81	4,153.77
Police	92,646.41	36,347.96	25,207.02	70,816.62	258,755.47
Fire	65,639.80	0	14,448.22	40,590.83	148,314.04
Inspections	9,612.52	490.31	3,177.66	8,927.31	32,619.32
Animal protection	732.38	0	0	0	0
Utilities-solid waste	33,781.15	4,282.00	6,414.82	18,021.79	65,849.48
Transportation	43,622.55	326.87	8,176.22	22,970.26	83,930.60
Human resources	31,217.81	0	6,129.19	17,219.34	62,917.41
Libraries	22,108.80	9,217.74	6,533.83	18,356.15	67,071.18
Environmental affairs	58,224.43	11,309.71	11,163.45	31,362.60	114,595.20

Allocated Central Service Costs for Fiscal Year Ended June 30, 1977

ORGANIZATIONS

Automotive Equipment F-1	Purchasing Division G-1	Printing Division H-1	Property I-1	Life Insurance L-1	J-1&K-1	Total
$ 0	$ 0	$ 1,721.22	$ 13,642.10	$ 0		$ 22,857.33
0	0	0	16,282.99	407.00		25,007.93
0	0	0	77,813.30	0		82,248.40
0	0	2,980.65	40,681.33	606.80		68,848.75
789.66	0	2,029.08	76,941.93	1,013.80		137,198.31
0	0	1,987.10	38,292.39	0		44,334.80
0	0	223.90	22,498.27	199.80		35,246.46
9,834.52	78.63	741.66	12,479.44	3,862.80		97,641.66
0	0	2,378.92	45,776.25	1,628.00		123,639.12
0	0	2,015.08	19,981.69	606.80		57,425.83
0	157.27	1,847.16	43,669.37	1,628.00		134,796.83
0	0	853.61	4,543.01	199.80		13,264.10
414.00	0	993.55	13,946.18	207.20		22,446.27
135,526.39	377.45	11,600.73	258,367.83	15,451.20		905,097.08
63,573.67	13,242.05	1,693.23	17,852.74	13,216.40		378,570.98
7,118.17	125.82	5,191.64	57,578.37	1,628.00		126,469.12
0	0	979.56	0	0		1,711.94
156,092.02	1,195.24	895.59	0	1,827.80		288,359.89
58,201.47	15,097.82	4,547.93	69,592.59	3,663.00		310,129.31
2,054.26	864.98	4,254.07	35,513.93	3,256.00		163,426.99
1,904.19	864.98	6,395.10	639.40	4,269.80		137,361.17
41,345.38	9,907.95	21,452.25	84,743.03	8,332.40		392,436.40

Table 5.1

CENTRAL SERVICE

Operating Department Schedule	Fiscal Analysis A-1	Data Analysis and Processing B-1	County Board C-1	County Manager D-1	Personnel Department E-1
Other Funds					
Public assistance	26,503.10	38,276.49	7,402.63	20,796.95	75,989.57
Utilities fund	6,957.64	35,628.85	12,198.87	34,271.50	125,223.97
Dog tax fund	503.51	0	178.52	501.53	1,832.54
Mental health services	1,007.03	0	345.14	969.63	3,542.92
Outside Agencies					
Retirement board		2,843.77			
Credit union		3,399.45			
Cigarette tax board		2,026.59			
Falls Church City		2,255.40			
Other allocations					
Subtotal	$457,739.19	$231,979.74	$119,013.33	$334,356.09	$1,221,697.23
Allocated to other central service agencies	0	94,890.41	0	0	0
Total allocation	$457,739.19	$326,870.15	$119,013.33	$334,356.09	$1,221,697.23
Allocated from other central service agencies	(59,394.19)	(26,938.15)	(21,077.33)	(96,441.09)	(577,168.23)
Totals—Central service costs	$398,345.00	$299,932.00	$ 97,936.00	$237,915.00	$ 644,529.00

(Continued)

ORGANIZATIONS

Automotive Equipment F-1	Purchasing Division G-1	Printing Division H-1	Property I-1	Life-Management Employees L-1	J-1&K-1	Total
3,891.41	0	6,059.25	6,350.52	4,876.60		190,146.52
48,402.10	8,586.89	2,588.82	32,433.27	6,711.80		313,003.71
1,027.62	0	27.99	0	0		4,071.71
0	0	531.76	322.18	407.00		7,125.66
						2,843.77
						3,399.45
						2,026.59
						2,255.40
		19,213.27	10,402.19			29,615.46
$530,174.86	$ 50,499.08	$103,203.12	$1,000,344.30	$74,000.00	$ 0	$4,123,006.94
0	106,769.92	36,733.31	164,877.70	0	907,020.00	1,310,291.34
$530,174.86	$157,269.00	$139,936.43	$1,165,222.00	$74,000.00	$907,020.00	$5,433,298.28
(274,975.92)	(4,623.00)	(35,262.43)	(140,411.00)	(74,000.00)	0	(1,310,291.34)
$255,198.94	$152,646.00	$104,674.00	$1,024,811.00	$ 0	$907,020.00	$4,123,006.94

Table 5.2 County Example: Transportation Department Indirect Cost Rate Proposal for Fiscal Year Ended June 30, 1977

Division/Activities	Total Costs	Unallowable Costs	Direct Costs Salaries and Wages	Direct Costs Fringe Benefits and Other	Indirect Costs
Division/Activities					
Project development	$ 628,306.00		$ 444,533.00	$ 183,773.00	
Operations	1,998,629.00		852,415.00	1,146,214.00	
Traffic engineering	596,212.00		335,050.00	261,162.00	
Systems planning and evaluation	742,782.00		237,849.00	504,933.00	
Department Indirect Costs					
Administration	107,228.00	$1523.00			$105,705.00
Subtotal	$4,073,157.00	$1523.00			
Central Service Cost Allocation Plan					
Exhibit A					310,129.31
Total cost	$4,383,286.31		$1,869,847.00	$2,096,082.00	$415,834.31

$$\text{Indirect costs} \quad \frac{\$415,834.31}{\$1,869,847.00} = 0.2224 = 22.24\%$$
Direct salaries and wages

82

ities preparing the long form plan may include indirect costs within the operating departments, while jurisdictions preparing the single-rate plan may not. The indirect costs within operating departments are generally the costs of the department director's office—for example, the sheriff's or police chief's office. Larger jurisdictions will find that these costs greatly increase their indirect cost rates as illustrated by the $105,705 departmental indirect costs shown in Table 5.2. Also, central service agency costs for such areas as data processing and printing that are charged to user agencies may not be included in the short form plan as indirect costs, but may be included under the long form method.

The ten steps described in this chapter are summarized here. The first two steps—choosing a basis for the plan and identifying the indirect cost areas—are identical to the first two for the simplified method outlined in Chapter 4.

1 Decide on the basis to be used for the preparation of the cost allocation plan.
2 Identify and list the indirect cost areas.
3 Choose an allocation basis for each indirect cost area.
4 Prepare a "Statement of Function and Benefit" for each central service agency.

5 Prepare explanations of central services billed to user agencies.

6 Identify allowable costs of indirect cost pools.

7 Compute depreciation on buildings and equipment and allocate the costs to the user agencies.

8 Determine the order in which the cost allocations will be made.

9 Allocate central service costs to operating agencies and other central service agencies.

10 Summarize all allocations to operating agencies.

The last step is the preparation of Table 5.1, which is easily constructed after completion of the other steps.

Examples from one city's and one county's cost allocation plans are extensively used in this section to illustrate the preparation steps. These examples should not be interpreted as the only ways of preparing the cost allocation plan, and alternatives available to local governments are highlighted, where appropriate.

PLAN PREPARATION STEPS

Step 1. Decide on the Basis to Be Used for Preparation of the Cost Allocation Plan

Budget or Financial Report

As discussed in Chapter 4, the Federal Guide OASC–10 permits jurisdictions to use their adopted budgets or most recent audited financial reports as bases for preparing the cost allocation plans. However, it is advisable for a jurisdiction to base its plan on the financial report after the first year. See Chapter 4, step 1 for a further discussion.

Step 2. Identify and List the Indirect Cost Areas

After completion of Step 1, the preparer may proceed to identify the allowable indirect cost areas within the following three categories:

- Central service agencies.
- Nondepartmental areas.
- Depreciation and use allowances.

Table 4.2 outlines the major allowable indirect cost

areas for local governments, and Table 4.3 outlines the major unallowable areas. As shown in Table 5.1, the allowable areas are listed across the top of the table.

Step 3. Choose an Allocation Basis for Each Indirect Cost Area

Example Allocation for Personnel Department

As discussed previously, the costs for each indirect cost pool identified in Table 4.2 are allocated or assigned separately to other agencies on some rational basis. The basis chosen should reflect the levels of services received by various agencies from the central service agency. An illustrative basis for a personnel department is "number of employees." In using this basis, one assumes that all employees of the local government receive approximately the same levels of services from the personnel department. For instance, in Table 5.3, the County Example's Department of Libraries has 113 employees or 5½% of the total number of employees in the county's operating agencies. It is therefore assumed that the Department of Libraries received almost 5½% of the Personnel Department's services; this percentage

**Table 5.3 County Example: Central Service Cost
Allocation Plan Personnel Department (1.1070)
Allocation of Costs for Fiscal Year Ended
June 30, 1977**

Operating Department	Number of Personnel	Percent	Allocation
Extension service	8	0.0039	$ 4,764.62
County attorney	8	0.0039	4,764.62
Circuit court	3	0.0015	1,832.55
District court	22	0.0107	13,072.16
Juvenile court	57	0.0277	33,841.01
County court clerks	2	0.0010	1,221.70
Commonwealth attorney	12	0.0058	7,085.84
Sheriff and jail	69	0.0335	40,926.86
Commissioner of revenue	53	0.0257	31,397.62
Real estate assessments	15	0.0073	8,918.39
Treasurer	45	0.0219	26,755.17
Electoral board	4	0.0019	2,321.22
Consumer affairs	7	0.0034	4,153.77
Police	436	0.2118	258,755.47
Fire	250	0.1214	148,314.04
Inspections	55	0.0267	32,619.32
Utilities–solid waste	111	0.0539	65,849.48
Transportation	141.4	0.0687	83,930.60
Human resources	106	0.0515	62,917.41
Libraries	113	0.0549	67,071.18
Environmental affairs	193	0.0938	114,595.20
Virginia public assistance	128	0.0622	75,989.57
Utilities	211	0.1025	125,223.97
Dog tax	3	0.0015	1,832.54
Mental health services board	6	0.0029	3,542.92
Total to be allocated	2058.4	1.0000	$1,221,697.23
Central service agencies	207		
Budget total	2265.4		

is applied to the Personnel Department's $1.2 million costs to yield $67,071.18 worth of services estimated to be provided by Personnel to Libraries.

Choice of the Best Possible Allocation Basis

The distribution basis chosen for an indirect cost area should be one that realistically reflects the level of services provided and also one that can be quantified readily. In choosing a basis, the availability of data should be considered carefully, and sometimes a less-than-ideal base may be chosen. OASC–10, p. 71, offers the following preface to its list of suggested bases for cost distribution:

The suggested bases are not mandatory for use if they are not suitable for the particular services involved. *Any method of distribution can be used which will produce an equitable distribution of cost.* In selecting one method over another, consideration should be given to the additional effort required to achieve a greater degree of accuracy. (Emphasis added.)

Example Cost Allocation

An example situation is the allocation of accounting costs among operating agencies. Although OASC–10 suggests "number of transactions processed" as a basis, one city did not have this data readily available by department. Therefore, the city used "budgeted departmental costs" for the allocation basis on the assumption that the basis does roughly reflect the volume of transactions performed by the accounting section of the finance office for the operating agencies. In making the allocation, however, the city did not include certain budget units—such as debt service and contingency accounts—in the allocation because these areas did not receive accounting services commensurate with the budget dollars. Because "total costs" is a rough measure, the basis should be used sparingly and only when the cost and effort required to collect alternate data are inordinately high.

Example Allocation Bases

Table 5.4 contains the allocation bases suggested in OASC–10 for selected cost areas, along with alternate bases that have been used by local governments. One caution regarding these allocation bases is this: several of the bases noted in the "Alternative" column are the direct charges made to agencies for the services. As discussed subsequently, costs charged directly to agencies may not be counted as indirect costs and included in the indirect cost pool. For in-

Table 5.4 Example Allocation Bases for Selected Indirect Cost Areas

Indirect Cost Pools	Allocation Bases Suggested in OASC–10[a]	Alternative Allocation Bases[b]
Accounting	Number of transactions processed	Total budget dollars[b]
Auditing	Direct audit hours	—
Bonding of employees	Number of employees covered	—
Budgeting	Direct hours of central budget employees	Total budget dollars[b]
Building depreciation	Not included	Gross floor area occupied
Building operations and maintenance	Gross floor area occupied	—
City/county manager or other chief executive	Not included	Number of employees or permanent positions
Data processing	Hours of usage	Direct charges to agencies
Garage		
Operations and maintenance	Number of miles driven or days used for vehicles assigned to agencies	Number of mechanic man-hours spent on vehicles assigned to agencies
Vehicle use allowance or depreciation	Not included	Vehicle-by-vehicle computation
Mail and messenger service	Number of documents handled or employees served	—
Payroll processing	Number of employees	
Personnel administration	Number of employees	Number of permanent positions
Printing and reproduction	Direct hours, pages printed, job basis	Direct charges made to agencies
Public information	Not included	Total budget dollars or number of employees
Purchasing/procurement	Number of transactions processed	Number of requisitions or purchase orders
Telephone	Number of telephone instruments	Number of telephone lines

[a] OASC–10, p. 71.

[b] "Total budget dollars" is an inaccurate basis and should be avoided, if possible.

90

stance, a jurisdiction's print shop might charge to agencies the costs of paper and other printing materials, but not those for labor, machine rental, supervisory, and other costs of the printing operation. The paper and other materials may not be included as indirect costs, but the relative amounts charged to agencies may be used as a basis for allocating all other costs of the print shop to user agencies as indirect costs.

Data Collection

After an allocation basis for each indirect cost area is chosen, the pertinent data may be collected. The amount of time required may vary greatly among the indirect cost areas. A purchasing department staff, for instance, may need to review their files to collect data on the "number of purchase orders by agency" for a given time period. On the other hand, the "number of personnel by agency" used to allocate personnel department costs is usually readily available. Any memorandums or worksheets used to help construct the bases should be retained by the jurisdiction.

Table 5.5 County Example: Central Service Cost Allocation Plan Statement of Function and Benefit Printing Division Department of Property Management For the Fiscal Year Ended June 30, 1977

The Printing Division is responsible for providing centralized printing and other services to all County departments and other non-County users. These services include operating the stationery stores that provide office supplies, providing Xerox and microfilming service. Printing and Xerox costs are billed to user County departments, while administration costs and other services are not.

All functions and services performed by the Printing Division benefit all County departments. Federal programs are benefited because application, grant awards, financial and performance reports, and other information about the programs must be printed, reproduced, or microfilmed for storage. Therefore, the costs of the Printing Division have been distributed to all County departments.

The basis for allocation is the ratio of monthly printing charges by departments. The base data were compiled by adding the actual charges billed to each department for all months in fiscal year 1976 for printing and Xeroxing costs. All departments receive essentially the same type and level of services. Hence, this base reflects this condition by distributing under recovered costs of providing these services to each department in proportion to its relative direct billed printing and Xeroxing charges. Additionally, base data are available, although not readily, and verifiable. The base data would be readily available if the County established one object code for recording all Printing Division costs.

**Table 5.6 City Example: Central Service Cost Allocation
Plan Statement of Function and Benefit
Personnel Department for the Fiscal Year
Ended June 30, 1978**

The Personnel Department is responsible for overall administration of the City's employment of City employees. This includes recruiting, interviewing, testing, and referring potential candidates to agencies for over 500 positions.

The Department has responsibility for classifying all City employees and maintaining and updating the City's classification schedule and pay plan. In addition, the Department oversees employee fringe benefits and the employee evaluation program.

All services performed by the Personnel Department benefit all departments of the City. The costs of the Department are, therefore, distributed to all City operating departments. Federal programs benefit from Personnel Department programs because the Department must classify new federally funded positions, recruit and test potential employees, and supervise the performance evaluation of those employees.

The basis for the allocation of costs is "number of employees." All employees receive essentially the same type and level of service. Therefore, this basis reflects this condition by distributing the total cost of providing these services to each department in proportion to each department's number of employees. The base data are readily available and verifiable.

Step 4. Prepare a "Statement of Function and Benefit" for Each Central Service Agency

Benefits Provided to Federal Programs

For each central service agency included in the indirect cost pool, a "Statement of Function and Benefit" must be prepared as shown in OASC–10, p. 52. The statement should summarize the agency's basic functions and describe how its services benefit federal grant programs. In addition, the statement should describe the allocation basis used for the distribution of the agency's costs and should explain why that basis was used. Illustrative statements from two jurisdictions are included as Tables 5.5 and 5.6

Step 5. Prepare Explanations of Central Services Billed to User Agencies

OASC–10 Requirement

This step fulfills the requirement in OASC–10, p. 53, that the plan include an explanation of all central service agency services directly billed to user agencies. The preparation of this summary, besides fulfilling the federal guide's requirement, will assist the preparer in identifying the direct-billed central service costs, which are unallowable indirect costs in the cost allocation plan.

Examples of Billed Services

1 One example of direct-billed central service agency costs is in the area of telephone service. A local government operating a Centrex telephone system might, for instance, charge operating agencies only for long distance calls and for the installation of telephones. All other costs of the system, including flat monthly charges, a central operator's salary, and basic system maintenance costs may be considered indirect costs for inclusion in the cost allocation plan.

2 A second example is data processing. A local government might charge only machine time and direct programming costs to users. Therefore, only such overhead costs as supervisors' salaries, building space, and machine maintenance may be included in the cost allocation plan as indirect costs. A jurisdiction should work toward charging data processing and other measurable services to user agencies, but until the 100% chargeout is achieved, the costs not billed to users should be treated as indirect costs. A jurisdiction attempting to charge central services to users will not jeopardize their federal grant reimbursement because direct-billed costs could be charged to some federal grants as direct charges. Alternatively, direct-billed costs could be included as departmental indirect costs as described in Chapter 6.

Format for Summary

A sample format for the summary of central services billed to users is shown in Table 5.7. Explanations of what costs are charged and the method of charging should be included. An important note contained in OASC–10, p. 53, is that selective billing of user agencies is not acceptable. In most cases if one agency is direct-billed for certain costs, then all user agencies should be billed for the same cost categories on the same basis.

Step 6. Identify Allowable Costs of Indirect Cost Pools

This step is probably the most time-consuming part of the plan preparation process because the budget

**Table 5.7 County Example: Central Service Cost
Allocation Plan Summary of Central Services
Billed to User Organizations**

Data processing	The local government operates a central computer center consisting of an IBM 370/135 Central Processing Unit and supporting equipment. The center provides both regular continuing and special job computer support to most operating and staff departments. Billings for service are made to user departments based on a standard price schedule. The price schedule is related to, and designed to recover, the costs of various types of jobs on each system. The pricing schedule is generally reviewed monthly and adjustments reflected in the following month's billing rates.[a] Costs consist of salaries and wages and fringe benefits of center operating personnel, supplies, maintenance, and equipment rental. Overhead costs are not included in the billing rate.
Auto equipment (motor pool)	The local government operates a central motor pool from a special fund that makes cars and trucks available to user departments. Receipts come from user departments that are billed monthly according to a schedule which reflects partial administrative and maintenance costs and partial use charges (depreciation costs) for each major class of equipment.

97

Table 5.7 (Continued)

Maintenance costs are reviewed monthly and the billing rate is changed yearly. Over or under recovery of costs are absorbed by appropriations from or returns to the general fund.[a] Such recoveries have averaged less than 6% of total expenditures for the past two years and less than 1% for the past year. The costs included are salaries and wages and fringe benefits of administrative and motor pool personnel, their travel, supplies, and parts and use charges for vehicles. Administrative and maintenance costs not recovered have been distributed to user departments on the basis of their respective monthly maintenance charges; and depreciation costs, calculated in accordance with FMC 74–4, have been distributed on the basis of the user department's respective monthly depreciation charges.

Printing   The local government operates a central printing plant which provides printing services to all user departments. Billings for services are made on a standard price schedule. The price schedule is related to, and designed to recover, the costs of various types of printing jobs. The price schedule takes into consideration the types of equipment, level of operator proficiency, and material used. The result is

Table 5.7 (Continued)

	an hourly rate by activity, consisting of operators' salaries and fringe benefits, an equipment use rate, and maintenance. Overhead support costs of the Division are not included in the price schedule. See Schedule H-2 for costs incurred, costs directly billed, and costs not recovered.[a] Use charges for equipment owned is determined in accordance with FMC 74–4.
Telephone	All long distance telephone calls are placed through a central switchboard and billed, with few exceptions, to the organizations making the call. All telephone installation charges are billed, with the same exceptions, to the organizations requesting telephone service. Basic telephone costs are billed directly to the Department of Human Resources, Sheriff and Jail, and other funds such as the Mental Health Board, Virginia Public Assistance fund, Retirement Board, and School Board. The billings consist of the actual monthly charges as rendered by the phone company.[a] No overhead support is included in the billings for basic telephone services.
Copying costs	The local government leases copying machines for use by County departments. The machines are equiped with a control panel that accepts plastic cards coded to

Table 5.7 (Continued)

	each user department. Copying costs are billed to user departments according to the number of copies made.[a]
Postage	The local government operates a central metered postage system that records actual postage costs by user departments. User departments are billed directly for metered postage.[a]
Office and operating supplies	The costs of supplies are billed directly to user departments.[a]

[a] The difference between costs billed to user agencies for data processing and automotive equipment and the actual costs incurred by users are adjusted in the subsequent year's billings. For instance, if the actual vehicle costs for Department A were $25,000 for fiscal 1979 and the billings, only $22,000, the additional $3,000 is billed to the Department in fiscal 1980. (An alternative to this adjustment method is to adjust the billings before the close of a fiscal year's books.)

and audit for a jurisdiction do not include the indirect cost pools as self-contained budget/accounting units. It is therefore necessary to evaluate separately each central service agency identified in Step 2 to determine whether part or all of the agency's costs may be allocated as indirect costs.

Step 6 involves the preparation of a schedule of "costs to be allocated" for each indirect cost pool. This schedule is a summary of the expenditures or budget figures for each area, with appropriate additions and subtractions, as subsequently described. The recommended format contained in OASC–10, Appendix 6, is followed here. This step is divided into six substeps, each representing a special type of indirect cost pool.

6a. Complete the "Costs to Be Allocated" Schedules for Indirect Cost Pools That Are Self-Contained Accounting/Budget Units

This is the least complex situation in which an entire budget unit comprises an allowable cost area.* The entire budget should be included in the schedule, separated into such major expenditure categories as follows:

• Salaries and wages.

* A "budget unit" has a separate transactional code in the jurisdiction's accounting system and usually covers a division of a department such as the accounting division of the finance department.

- Fringe benefits.

- Travel and training.

- Materials and supplies.

- Contractual services.

- Equipment and other.

- Capital outlay.

Examples

Tables 5.8 and 5.9 provide "costs to be allocated" schedules for the City Example's Public Information Office and the County Example's Fiscal Analysis Division. The figures in these schedules are extracted directly from the jurisdictions' financial documents.

6b. For Each Central Service Agency Providing More than One Type of Service, Enter the Costs of Each Major Service of the Agency on a Separate "Costs to Be Allocated" Schedule

The units of a central service agency may be referred to as divisions, sections, activities, programs, or

**Table 5.8 City Example: Central Service Cost Allocation
Plan Department of Public Information (01–130)
Costs to Be Allocated for Fiscal Year
Ended June 30, 1978**

Salaries and wages		$40,834
Fringe benefits		5,779
Materials and supplies		4,225
Travel and training		750
Contractual services		17,403
Equipment		350
Total		$69,341
Less unallowable costs		
Capital outlay	$ 350	
Costs chargeable to federal grant[a]	14,595	−14,945
Plus costs allocated from		
other schedules		
Computer services	$ 591	
Printing and mail room	2,451	3,042
Total costs to be allocated		$57,438

[a] Budgeted as reimbursement from the U.S. Department of Housing and Urban Development (Community Development program).

other designations. The inclusion of the costs on separate schedules for the units is necessary because the costs of the central service functions are allocated separately for different allocation bases.

**Table 5.9 County Example: Central Service Cost
Allocation Plan Fiscal Analysis Division (1.1031)
Department of Management Systems and Budget
Costs to Be Allocated for Fiscal Year Ended
June 30, 1977 Based on Fiscal Year 1977
Approved Budget**

Salaries and wages		$251,705
Fringe benefits		67,240
Contractual services		90,280
Material and supplies		4,900
Equipment		0
Total		$414,125
Less unallowable costs		
Capital outlay	$ 0	
Costs chargeable to		
CETA grant	15,780	15,780
Subtotal		$398,345.00
Add allocated costs from		
Data Analysis	$38,472.62	
Printing Division	4,002.18	
Property Division	16,919.39	59,394.19
Total costs to be		
allocated		$457,739.19

For instance, the County Example's Property
Management Department includes these five divisions: automotive equipment, printing, purchasing,

property (building operation and maintenance), and the office of the director.* Each of these division's costs, including the director's office, is listed on a separate "costs to be allocated" schedule. Step 6e explains the handling of the director's office costs.

6c. Eliminate from Central Service Agency Divisions the Costs of Functions not Allowable in Indirect Cost Pools. Enter Allowable Costs only on a "Costs to Be Allocated" Schedule

In addition to their allowable functions, some central service agencies perform functions not allowable in indirect cost pools. Ideally, a jurisdiction's financial management system provides an activity breakdown of expenditures on specific functions performed by an agency, and the budget mirrors the breakdown. If so, it is not difficult to include only allowable costs areas on the "costs to be allocated" schedule. If a portion of a central service agency is deleted because it is unallowable, this unallowable activity must be included as an operating agency to which indirect costs will be allocated.

* It may be necessary to separate a division into smaller units if its activities are varied. *See* Step 9 of this chapter for a further discussion.

Example of Nonallowable Function

A breakdown that may be required is a finance office that performs accounting, disbursing of funds, and budgeting, which all may be allowable functions, in addition to tax collection, an unallowable indirect cost area. If a jurisdiction's accounting and budgeting system does not separate tax collection from the other functions, it may be necessary to prepare a breakdown of each individual's salary and fringe benefits, as well as each nonpersonnel line item to separate allowable from unallowable costs. If one employee performs several functions, any salary breakdown for that individual should be based on timesheets kept by the individual for an adequately long and representative time period to reflect a realistic distribution.

Nondepartmental Costs

Nondepartmental costs such as Workmen's Compensation, bonding of employees, and insurance should be separated from nonallowable costs for contributions to community organizations, and contingencies, and so on. Nondepartmental cost items may be combined on the same "costs to be allocated" schedule if they have the same allocation basis. But if bonding of employees is allocated on the basis of the employees actually covered by the policies and Workmen's Compensation is allocated on the basis of the total number of employees, these cost areas should be included on separate schedules.

6d. Deduct Unallowable Costs from the Indirect Cost Pools

On completion of Step 6c, each indirect cost pool should have a "costs to be allocated" schedule containing all of its costs. As Table 5.8 shows, the costs are added to yield a subtotal to which additional adjustments will be made. One adjustment is the deletion of any costs from the indirect cost pool from these three major categories:

- Capital costs, including equipment.

- Costs charged directly to federal grants.

- Costs billed directly to users.

**Table 5.10 County Example: Central Service Cost
Allocation Plan Printing Division (1.1065)
Property Management Department Costs to Be
Allocated for Fiscal Year Ended June 30, 1977
Based on Fiscal Year 1977 Approved Budget**

Salaries and wages		$174,831
Fringe benefits		48,028
Contractual services		74,123
Materials and supplies		81,800
Equipment		8,100
Total		$386,882
Less		
Capital outlay	$ 8,100	
Costs directly billed	273,000	
Chargeable to CETA	10,438	291,538
Total		$ 95,344
Add		
Use charge for equipment,		
Schedule H–4		9,330
		104,674
Add		
Cost allocated from		
Property management		
director (Table 5.12)	7,121.00	
Property division	28,141.43	35,262.43
Costs to be allocated		
on Schedule H–1		$139,936.43

Example Deletions

Table 5.10 presents three unallowable deductions from the County Example Printing Division's "costs to be allocated" schedule. The $8,100 for equipment, the $273,000 of printing supplies and direct labor charged to users, and the $10,438 chargeable to CETA are all deducted from the Printing Division's total budget of $386,882. The County Example parallels the format shown in Appendix 6 of this guide, as recommended in OASC–10.

6e. Establish a "Costs to Be Allocated" Schedule for the Administrative Division of Each Central Service Agency and Allocate These Costs to the Subunits of the Agency

This optional step is for a jurisdiction with an "administrative division" or "office of the director" established as a separate accounting/budget unit within a central service agency. The preparer constructs a "costs to be allocated" schedule for all administrative division costs and then allocates these costs to the department's divisions, usually on the basis of the number of personnel working in the divisions. These costs will then in turn be allocated again to the agencies benefiting from the activities of the central service divisions.

Example for Property Management Department

An example is the county's Property Management Department that has five divisions, plus the director's office. The costs to be allocated for this office are included in Table 5.11, and the allocation of this $50,361 is shown in Table 5.12. These amounts are added to the costs to be allocated schedules for these divisions, as illustrated in Table 5.10 for the Printing Division. The $7121 of the director's office's costs

Table 5.11 County Example: Central Service Cost Allocation Plan Property Management Director (1.1061) Property Management Department Costs to Be Allocated for Fiscal Year Ended June 30, 1977

Salaries and wages	$39,696
Fringe benefits	9,320
Contractual services	1,345
Materials and supplies	0
Equipment	0
Total costs to be allocated	$50,361

Table 5.12 County Example: Central Service Cost Allocation Plan Property Management Director (1.1061) Property Management Department Allocation of Costs to Divisions for Fiscal Year Ended June 30, 1977

Department Divisions	Number of Personnel	Percent	Allocation
Property	34	32.08	$16,156
Purchasing	4	3.78	1,904
Central stores	5	4.72	2,377
Printing (Table 5.10)	15	14.14	7,121
Equipment	48	45.28	22,803
Total allocated	106	100.00	$50,361

are included in this table as an addition to the Printing Division's budget. The other additions to the budget—the use charge for equipment and the Property Division costs—are discussed in steps 7 and 8, which follow.

Step 7. Compute Depreciation on Buildings and Equipment and Allocate the Costs to the User Agencies

All indirect costs identified in the cost allocation plan derive from a jurisdiction's budget or financial report, with one exception—depreciation. Even though depreciation should not, under generally accepted accounting principles, be recorded in a local government's general accounting records, depreciation may be computed and included as an indirect cost pool.*

Definition of Depreciation

Depreciation cost is a portion of the original cost of a fixed asset that is considered an expense for a current period, usually one year. The following describes the federal guide's requirements for computation of depreciation, with examples included for the major types of assets to be depreciated.

Requirements for Depreciation

These are the OASC–10 requirements regarding depreciation:

- Allowable Assets for Depreciation. Buildings and equipment, including motor vehicles, are allow-

* National Committee on Governmental Accounting, *Governmental Accounting, Auditing, and Financial Reporting* (Chicago: Municipal Finance Officers Association, 1968), p. 11.

able items. Land, idle facilities, and unusable equipment may not be included.

- Basis for Computation. The acquisition cost must be the basis for computing depreciation, supported by actual cost records or, when such are unavailable, by a reasonable estimate of the original acquisition cost. The basis for the estimate should be explained in the working papers.

- Depreciation Method. The straight-line method of computing depreciation generally should be used.* The computation involves (1) taking the cost of the asset, (2) subtracting an estimated salvage value, and (3) prorating the cost equally over the estimated service life of the asset. For example, annual depreciation on a local government building estimated to have a useful life of 45 years would be computed as follows, using the straight-line method:

Original cost	$1,100,000
Less estimated salvage value†	− 110,000
Equals base for depreciation	$ 990,000
Divided by useful life	÷ 45 years
Equals annual depreciation	$ 22,000

* *See* OASC–10, pp. 22 and 40.
† Salvage value at the end of 45 years.

- Alternative to Depreciation. OASC–10 permits an alternative to depreciation known as a "use allowance." For buildings, the annual allowance may not exceed 2% of the original acquisition cost; for equipment, the allowance may not exceed 6 ⅔ %.

- Consistency in Treatment of Assets. Each category of assets must be treated consistently. For instance, if the use allowance is applied to one building, then it must be used on all buildings.

- Federally Funded Assets. Any equipment or buildings financed through federal grant funds or donated by the federal government must be excluded from the computation of the depreciation or use allowance. However, jurisdictions do not need to exclude fixed assets purchased with Federal Revenue Sharing funds or Anti-Recession Fiscal Assistance funds.

3 Examples

1 Buildings. Buildings owned and occupied by the local government may be depreciated using the straight-line method, or the use allowance of 2% may be applied to their original purchase or con-

Table 5.13 City Example: Central Service Cost Allocation Plan Schedule I-4 General Services: Building Operation and Maintenance (01–726–7083) Calculation and Allocation of Building Depreciation

Calculation of Depreciation

Formula (straight-line depreciation): $\dfrac{\text{original cost} - \text{salvage value}}{\text{estimated service life}} = \text{annual depreciation}$

Facility	Construction/ Purchase Date	Building Construction/ Purchase Cost		Less Salvage Value		Equals Base for Depreciation		Divided by Estimated Useful Life (years)		Equals Annual Depreciation
Brotherhood Recreation Center	1973	$ 363,213	−	$ 36,000	=	$327,213	÷	20	=	$16,360
South Liberty Street Recreation Center	1969	385,531	−	38,000	=	347,531	÷	20	=	17,377
Woodland Heights Recreation Center	1968	159,788	−	16,000	=	143,788	÷	20	=	7,189
Municipal Building	1971	80,000[a]	−	8,000	=	72,000	÷	45	=	1,600
City Hall	1960	1,063,476	−	106,000	=	957,476	÷	45	=	21,277
Garage (new sections)	1975	150,399	−	0	=	150,399	÷	20	=	7,520

Table 5.13 (Continued)
Allocation of Depreciation

	Ft²	Percent	Depreciation Allocation
City Hall (allocation based on square footage occupied by agencies)			
Mayor and city council	1,591	3.41	$ 726
City manager	816	1.75	372
Fire	10,896	23.39	4,977
Police	20,991	45.05	9,585
Civil defense	2,193	4.71	1,002
Communications	1,878	4.03	857
Public works	3,252	6.98	1,485
Community development and planning	2,823	6.06	1,289
Finance: Collection and city clerk	861	1.85	395
Finance: Accounting	1,290	2.77	589
Total to be allocated	46,591	100.00	$21,277
General services and central service agencies	15,523		
Total	62,114		

Parks and Recreation Department Buildings

Brotherhood Recreation Center	$16,360
South Liberty Street Recreation Center	17,377
Woodland Heights Recreation Center	7,189
Municipal Building	1,600
Total annual depreciation	$42,526

General Services Department, Garage Division Building

Annual depreciation—Garage	$7,520

ᵃ Municipal building cost estimated.

struction cost. Table 5.13 shows depreciation cost computed and allocated in four steps, which one must perform as follows:

a Determine the construction or purchase date and the cost to the local government of the building. This cost should include improvements to the building.

b Subtract an estimated salvage value for the building at the end of its useful life as a local government building to arrive at the depreciation base.

c Determine the useful life for each building, and divide this into the depreciation base. The U.S. Internal Revenue Service provides guidelines for the years of useful life of various types of buildings (for instance, 45 years for an office building), but local government officials and builders should also be consulted to estimate the useful life of the buildings.

d Allocate the depreciation costs to the users of the buildings. As shown at the bottom of Table 5.13, the city hall space is allocated to users on the basis of the square feet occupied by the agencies, and the recreation buildings and garage are allocated to the respective users. The common space—such as restrooms, plant operations areas, and hallways—represents a large portion of the 15,523 ft² not used to allocate the costs.

Table 5.14 City Example: Central Service Cost Allocation Plan General Services Department: Garage (01–726–7084) Calculation of Use Charge on Automotive Equipment[a]

	Original Cost of Equipment	Less Federally Funded Equipment	Equals Net Cost of Equipment to City	Times Use Charge Rate of 6⅔%	Equals Use Charge to Be Allocated
Operating Agency					
Community development	$ 20,532	$ 2,569	$ 17,963	0.0667	$ 1,198
Car pool	19,226	8,488	10,738	0.0667	716
General services: airport	4,093	—	4,093	0.0667	273
Parks and recreation	48,193	—	48,193	0.0667	3,214
Public works	1,123,744	12,917	1,110,827	0.0667	74,092
Police	145,675	21,324	124,351	0.0667	8,294
Fire	277,699	—	277,699	0.0667	18,523
Communications	6,057	—	6,057	0.0667	404
Total operating agencies	$1,645,219	$45,298	$1,599,921		$106,714
Central Service Agency					
City manager	$ 4,455	—	$ 4,455	0.0667	$ 297
Public information	4,287	4,287	0	0.0667	0
Garage	12,266	—	12,266	0.0667	818
Building maintenance	1,672	—	1,672	0.0667	112
Total central service agencies	$ 22,680	$ 4,287	$ 18,393		$ 1,227
Total to be allocated	$1,667,899	$49,585	$1,618,314		$107,941

[a] From "Fiscal 1978 Automotive Equipment Fleet List" as of November 1, 1977.

Use Allowance on Motor Vehicles

2 Motor Vehicles. Because of the difficulty of computing depreciation for each motor vehicle owned by the jurisdiction, the use allowance of 6⅔% should be used as a substitute. These steps are required for the example provided in Table 5.14:

a Determine the original cost of the motor vehicles assigned to each agency, including central service agencies. Only vehicles currently in use may be included.

b Identify the vehicles funded by federal grants. Subtract the federal funding from the original equipment cost to yield the net local cost of the equipment to the jurisdiction.

c Multiply 0.0667 (6⅔%) times the net cost for each agency to yield the use allowance (use charge). Computation of the use allowance by agency is recommended because this prevents the need for further allocation of the costs.

Use Allowances on Other Equipment

3 Other Equipment. Local government-owned equipment other than motor vehicles may be included in the cost allocation plan, preferably by applying the use allowance of 6⅔%. If the jurisdiction has a good fixed asset inventory, computation of the use allowance on such equipment as furniture and typewriters should be considered. However, the small amount of the use allowance for these items may not justify the effort required for the computation. A class of equipment commonly included in cost allocation plans is printing equipment, for which an example of use allowance computation is shown in Table 5.15.

Table 5.15 County Example: Central Service Cost Allocation Plan Printing Division (1.1065) Property Management Department Calculation of Depreciation for Fiscal Year Ended June 30, 1977

Original cost of printing equipment[a]	$139,880
Use charge of 6²/₃%	×0.0667
Equipment use charge to be allocated	$ 9,330

[a] None of the equipment was federally funded.

Depreciation or use allowance costs may be included in the cost allocation plan summary as separate indirect cost pools or may be combined with the costs of appropriate central service agencies—for example, motor vehicle use allowances with the vehicle maintenance and operation costs. A third alternative is to include the use allowance with other "departmental indirect costs" on the indirect cost proposal. Depreciation and use allowance costs will be discussed further under Step 9, which covers allocations to agencies.

Step 8. Determine the Order in Which the Cost Allocations Will Be Made

*Cross-Allocation among
Central Service Agencies*

Certain central service agencies provide a significant level of services to other central service agencies. For example, a jurisdiction's data processing department probably provides a high level of services to the finance department. Therefore, a portion of the indirect costs from the data processing department should be included with other finance department costs to be allocated. The indirect costs of the data processing department are then allocated again to users of the finance department's services.

Selective Allocations among
Central Service Agencies

A problem with this cross-allocation process is that if all central service agency costs were allocated to all other central service agencies, there would be no starting point. One central service agency's costs would be allocated back to itself. Also, because the levels of services provided by central service agencies to each other are in many cases minimal, cross-allocations often make little difference in the final indirect cost rates. Therefore, this guide recommends that only the costs of selected central service agencies be allocated to other central service agencies. The recommended guideline is this: allocate indirect costs from Central Service Agency A to Central Service Agency B only if the level of services provided represents a significant portion of Agency A's operation.

Examples

The following examples should assist in explaining the guideline:

1 One-third of a jurisdiction's data processing operation is devoted to providing services to the finance

department as measured by computer time. The data processing costs should be allocated to the finance department and other user agencies.

2 A jurisdiction's purchasing department provides to the city garage two-thirds of its total procurement services as measured by the number of purchase orders issued. This is another example of a cross-allocation that should be performed.

3 A printing division has only 15 of a jurisdiction's total 2200 employees or less than 1%. Thus for the personnel department, the chief executive's office, and other central service agencies for which "number of personnel" is used as an allocation basis, the cost allocations should not be made to the printing division because of the division's small number of employees.

Determining the Allocation Order

Because of the cross-allocation process, it is important that allocations be performed in the proper sequence. Therefore, it is recommended that the form in Table 5.16, or a similar one, be completed to plan which central service agencies' costs will be allocated to other agencies and to plan the order for the allocations. This form, which is not required by OASC–10, is constructed and used as follows:

Table 5.16 City Example: Allocation of Central Service Agency Costs to Other Central Service Agencies[a]

Allocation Order:	8	1	9	2	10	11	3	12	7	4	5	6
				Costs Allocated to these Central Service Agencies								
Central Service Agencies	City Manager	Management and Budget	Public Information	Community Relations	Personnel	Finance	Telephone	Garage	Buildings	Purchasing	Printing	Computer Services
City manager	x											
Management and budget		x										
Public information			x									
Community relations				x								
Personnel					x							
Finance						x						-
Telephone							x					
Garage and vehicle use allowance								x				
Building O and M and depreciation	yes					yes		yes	x			
Purchasing										x		
Printing and mail			yes		yes			yes			x	
Computer services			yes		yes	yes		yes	yes			x

[a] See the text for an example of this table.

1 Place the names of the central service agencies across the top and the left side of the form.

2 Indicate on the form which agencies in the left column will have their costs allocated to the agencies across the top of the form. The allocations indicated on Table 5.16 are the following for a city:

- Personnel department costs allocated to the garage because of the large number of employees working on the garage.
- Building operation and maintenance and building depreciation to the city manager's office and other agencies because of the large floor space occupied by those agencies.
- Purchasing to the garage because of the large number of purchase orders generated by the garage.
- Printing and mail room to public information and personnel because of the large volume of printing performed by these agencies.
- Computer services to five central service agencies that comprise the computer services department's principal "customers."

3 Establish an appropriate order for the allocations by entering a number above each agency listed across the top of the chart. The column for each agency must be scanned to make sure that no further allocations are required before that agency's costs can be allocated. For example, the preparer notes in the first column of Table 5.16 that the City Manager's Office must have building "O and M" and depreciation allocated to it, so he moves to the next column. Number 1 is assigned to the Management and Budget Office, because no allocations must be made to that agency. Accordingly, numbers 2 through 6 may be assigned to the five other agencies that will not receive allocations from other offices. Building "O and M" costs may be allocated next (7) after Computer Services has been allocated; the costs of the City Manager's Office may be allocated next (8), and so on. On completion of this table, the preparer may proceed to Step 9 for the cost allocations. See Appendix 7 for an alternate cost allocation method—the "step-down" method.

Step 9. Allocate Central Service Costs to Operating Agencies and Other Central Service Agencies

For each indirect cost pool, a schedule entitled "allocation of costs" must be prepared. The four basic steps required for preparation of this schedule are listed and described here.

9a. List All Agencies to Which Indirect Costs Will Be Allocated, and List Separately Other Agencies to Which Costs Will Not Be Allocated

Table 5.17 shows an "allocation of costs" schedule for a purchasing department. All agencies receiving services from the Purchasing Department are listed on the schedule, with all agencies to have indirect costs allocated to them included in the top half of the schedule. The agencies to be "burdened" in this example include these:

- Operating agencies such as Police, Fire, and Public Works.

- One central service agency—the Garage.

- Central service divisions not providing functions allowable as indirect cost pools—Tax Collection, City Clerk and Airport.

Cost Areas Not Burdened

The central service agencies other than the Garage are not burdened because of the relatively small number of requisitions (the basis for the allocation)

Table 5.17 City Example: Central Service Cost Allocation Plan General Services Department: Purchasing (01-726-7082) Allocation of Costs for Fiscal Year Ended June 30, 1978

	Number of Requisitions[a]	Percent	Allocation
Fire	36	0.99	$ 576
Police	72	1.99	1,158
Civil defense	24	0.66	384
Communications	96	2.65	1,542
Public works	432	11.92	6,936
Parks and recreation	336	9.27	5,394
Community development and planning	252	6.96	4,050
Finance: Collection and city clerk	24	0.66	384
General services: Airport	24	0.66	384
General services: Garage	2328	64.24	37,376
Total to be allocated	3624	100.00	$58,184[b]

Table 5.17 (Continued)

	Number of Requi- sitions[a] Percent	Allocation
Other Central Service Agencies[c]		
City manager	8	
Management and budget	27	
Public information	9	
Community relations	5	
Personnel	37	
Finance: Accounting	33	
General services: Building	43	
Computer services	4	
Subtotal other central service agencies	166	
Total requisitions	3790	

[a] A three month sample of requisitions by agency is used as the allocation basis.
[b] Allocated from Table 5.19.
[c] Central Service Agencies other than the Garage are not burdened because of the relatively small number of requisitions they generate.

generated by them. It may be necessary to exclude from the allocation process cost areas other than

**Table 5.18 County Example: Central Service Cost
Allocation Plan Fiscal Analysis Division (1.1031)
Department of Management Systems and Budget
Allocation of Costs for Fiscal Year
Ended June 30, 1977**

Operating Department	Total Fiscal Year 1977 Approved Department Costs	Percent	Allocation
Extension service	$ 90,493	0.0021	$ 961.25
County attorney	167,036	0.0030	1,785.18
Circuit court	178,701	0.0042	1,922.50
District court	594,447	0.0139	6,362.58
Juvenile court	936,220	0.0219	10,024.49
Court clerks	220,668	0.0052	2,380.24
Commonwealth attorney	243,520	0.0057	2,609.11
Sheriff and jail	1,328,055	0.0311	14,235.69
Commissioner of revenue	879,830	0.0206	9,429.43
Real estate assessment	353,575	0.0083	3,799.24
Treasurer	840,088	0.0196	8,971.69
Electoral board	140,257	0.0033	1,510.54
Consumer affairs	111,015	0.0026	1,190.12
Police	8,656,767	0.2024	92,646.41
Fire	6,131,206	0.1434	65,639.80
Inspections	899,879	0.0210	9,612.52
Animal protection	68,602	0.0016	732.38
Utilities-solid waste	3,155,537	0.0738	33,781.15

Table 5.18 (Continued)

Operating Department	Total Fiscal Year 1977 Approved Department Costs	Percent	Allocation
Transportation	4,073,157	0.0953	43,622.55
Human resources	2,915,019	0.0682	31,217.81
Libraries	2,064,144	0.0483	22,108.80
Environmental affairs	5,438,022	0.1272	58,224.43
Public assistance[a]	2,478,037	0.0579	26,503.10
Utilities fund– administration[a]	651,048	0.0152	6,957.64
Dog tax	48,702	0.0011	503.51
Mental health services board[a]	94,594	0.0022	1,007.03
Total to be allocated	$42,758,619	1.0000	$457,739.19
Not Burdened			
Central service organizations[a]	8,224,884		
Debt service[c]	12,365,249		
Regional contributions[c]	1,106,783		
Bus subsidy[c]	160,000		
Public assistance– payouts[a]	6,965,041		

131

Table 5.18 (Continued)

Operating Department	Total Fiscal Year 1977 Approved Department Costs	Percent	Allocation
Mental health board–payouts[a]	855,919		
Transportation commission[c]	375,000		
Capital outlay[c]	549,786		
Utilities fund[a]	9,577,519		
Fiscal year 1977 budget total	$82,938,800		

[a] These three special funds do not receive Fiscal Analysis benefits (budgeting and accounting) commensurate with their total approved costs. Fiscal Analysis activities are generally confined to the administrative costs of the three funds. The balances of the three funds represent payouts or operations for which little central budgeting or accounting services are rendered with most budgeting and accounting services performed within the three funds.

[b] Central Service organizations are not burdened because the allocated costs would be reallocated to operating departments.

[c] These activities are not burdened with Fiscal Analysis costs because the activities are performed by central service organizations which are not burdened.

central service agencies in some cases. For example, where "total budget dollars" or "total expenditures" is used as a basis for allocating a finance department or other central service agency's costs, it may be logical to delete certain cost areas from the allocation. Table 5.18 is an example of an office providing accounting and budgeting services. It shows that such items as debt service, regional contributions, and welfare payouts are excluded from the allocation because "these special funds do not receive Fscal Analysis benefits (budgeting and accounting) commensurate with their total approved costs" (see the first footnote to Table 5.18).

Separate Listing of Agencies

Each agency operating federally funded programs should be separately listed on the "allocation of costs" schedule. Other operating agencies without federal programs may be summarized on one line, as shown in Appendix 8 of this guide, from OASC–10. Such a summary may not save the preparer a significant amount of time, since the allocation basis data must be collected agency by agency. Therefore, this guide recommends that all the jurisdiction's major departments be listed separately and that only the smallest agencies not operating federal programs be summarized on one line.

9b. List the Units to Be Used for the Allocation Basis

As illustrated in Table 5.17 the allocation units are listed in the first column. A subtotal is drawn for those agencies receiving allocations.

9c. Compute the Percentages of the Allocation Units by Agency

Table 5.17's second column contains the percentages of the allocation units for the agencies that will receive allocations.

9d. Allocate the Indirect Costs from the "Costs to Be Allocated Schedule" on the Basis of the Allocation Percentages

This step requires entering the total amount from the "costs to be allocated" schedule onto the "allocation

**Table 5.19 City Example: Central Service
Cost Allocation Plan General Services
Department: Purchasing (01-726-7082)
Costs to Be Allocated for Fiscal Year
Ended June 30, 1978**

Salaries and wages	$20,801
Fringe benefits	3,245
Materials and supplies	600
Travel and training	170
Contractual services	516
Equipment	0
Total	$25,332
Plus general services department administration costs allocated on Table 5.20	32,852
Total costs to be allocated	$58,184

of costs" schedule and distributing the costs among
the agencies on the basis of the allocation percentages. For example, the $58,184 of costs to be allo-
cated for the Purchasing Department is taken from
Table 5.19, entered in the third column of Table
5.17 and allocated according to the percentages in
the second column.

Allocations to Central Service Agencies

Indirect costs allocated to other central service agen-

Table 5.20 City Example: Central Service Cost Allocation Plan General Services Department: Garage (01-726-7084) Costs to Be Allocated for Fiscal Year Ended June 30, 1978

	Operation and Maintenance Cost	Depreciation Cost
Salaries and wages	$160,585	
Fringe benefits	27,258	
Materials and supplies	7,425	
Travel and training	1,435	
Contractual services	11,845	
Equipment	1,600	
Total	$210,148	
Less unallowable costs: capital outlay	1,600	
Plus costs allocated from other schedules		
Personnel department	$ 2,684	
Computer services	1,478	
General services department Purchasing (Table 5.17)	37,376	
General services department Administration	16,426	
General services department Building operation and maintenance	10,558	68,522
Depreciation cost on vehicles		$105,998
Total costs to be allocated	$277,070	$105,998

cies should be added to the "costs to be allocated" schedules of those agencies. In the Purchasing Division example (Table 5.17), the $37,376 allocated to the Garage is added at the bottom of Table 5.20. For the Garage, a total of $68,522 from other schedules, including the $37,376 from the Purchasing Division, is added to the agency's operational costs to yield the Garage's total of $277,070 costs to be allocated.

Further Examples

The Purchasing Division example used to illustrate the cost allocations is a simple case that requires the minimum amount of work. Additional examples presented in the next section include suggested methods for handling more complicated allocations.

Case A. Allocation of Building-Related Costs

A recommended method of handling building space costs is to compute and allocate the depreciation (or use allowance) costs separately from the building "O and M" costs, and then to combine these costs on

Table 5.21 City Example: Central Service Cost Allocation Plan General Services: Building Operation and Maintenance (01–726–7083) Costs to Be Allocated for Fiscal Year Ending June 30, 1978

		Operation and Mainte- nance Cost	Depreci- ation Cost
Salaries and wages		$ 53,188	
Fringe benefits		9,250	
Materials and supplies		39,300	
Travel and training		300	
Contractual services		69,731	
Equipment and construction		15,050	
Debt service		52,361	
Total		$239,180	
Less unallowable costs			
Capital outlay	$15,050		
Debt service	52,361	−67,411	
Plus costs from other schedules General services department administration	20,533		
Computer services	1,182	+21,715	
Depreciation cost to be allocated			$71,323
Total costs to be allocated in Table 5.23		$193,484	$71,323

Table 5.22 City Example: Central Service Cost Allocation Plan
General Services: Building Operation and Maintenance (01–726–7088)
Allocation of Operation and Maintenance Costs[a]

	Gross Floor Area (ft²)						
	City Hall	Garage Office Space	Municipal Building	Airport	Total	Percent	Allocation
Mayor and city council	1,591				1,591	2.08	$ 4,024
City manager	816				816	1.07	2,070
Fire	10,896				10,896	14.24	27,552
Police	20,991				20,991	27.43	53,073
Civil defense	2,193				2,193	2.87	5,553
Communications	1,878				1,878	2.45	4,740
Public works	3,252				3,252	4.25	8,223
Community Development and planning	2,823				2,823	3.69	7,140
Finance: Collection and clerk	861				861	1.13	2,186
Finance: Accounting	1,290				1,290	1.69	3,270
General services: Airport				19,879	19,879	25.98	50,267
General services: Garage		1,200			1,200	1.57	3,038
Parks and recreation			8,844		8,844	11.55	22,348
Total to be allocated	46,591	1,200	8,844	19,879	76,514	100.00	$193,484
General services and other central service agencies	15,523				15,523		
Total	62,114	1,200	8,844	19,879	92,037		

[a] List of square footage for City agencies' offices prepared by the General Services Director (as of December 1977). See worksheets.

139

one summary schedule. Table 5.13 shows the computation and the allocation of the depreciation costs of six local government-owned buildings, including city hall. Depreciation on the four recreation buildings is all assigned to the Parks and Recreation Department; depreciation on the garage is assigned to the Garage Division; and depreciation on city hall is allocated according to the space occupied by the agencies. The total depreciation is shown on Table 5.21, the "costs to be allocated" schedule, and is allocated on Table 5.23. The operation and maintenance costs for the buildings are allocated on the basis of the relative space occupied in buildings operated and maintained by the General Services Department. As shown in Table 5.22, three of the recreation buildings are excluded from the computation because they are maintained and operated through the Parks and Recreation Department's budget. Therefore, the 76,514 ft^2 in the buildings maintained and operated by the General Services Department are used as the allocation units for distributing the $193,484 in "O and M" costs. Finally, the $193,484 is added agency by agency to the $71,323 in depreciation costs on Table 5.23 to yield the total building space costs. The combination of depreciation/use allowance costs with "O and M" costs on one schedule is also recommended for motor vehicles, so that the cost column included on the final

Table 5.23 City Example: Central Service Cost Allocation Plan Schedule I-1 General Services: Building Operation and Maintenance (01–726–7083) Summary of Allocated Costs

	Operation and Maintenance Costs (Table 5.21)	Building Depreciation (Table 5.13)	Total Costs
Mayor and city council	$ 4,024	$ 726	$ 4,750
City manager	2,070	372	2,442
Fire	27,552	4,977	32,529
Police	53,073	9,585	62,658
Civil defense	5,553	1,002	6,555
Communications	4,740	857	5,597
Public works	8,223	1,485	9,708
Community development and planning	7,140	1,289	8,429
Finance: Collection and clerk	2,186	395	2,581
Finance: Accounting	3,270	589	3,859
General services: Airport	50,267	0	50,267
General services: Garage	3,038	7,520	10,558
Parks and recreation	22,348	42,526	64,874
Total allocation	$193,484 +	$71,323 =	$264,807

cost allocation plan includes all costs to the local government of the motor vehicles.

Case B. Central Service Agencies Providing Various Functions

As discussed in Step 6b, it may be necessary to divide certain central service agencies into smaller "pieces" because they provide a variety of functions. Separating the Property Management Department into its divisions, as described previously, may not be a small enough breakdown. An example is the Printing Division that operates a postage meter for all agencies, provides interoffice mail service, and handles the central stores' operation for office supplies, in addition to its basic printing and duplicating function. Because of the variety of functions provided by the Division, it may be desirable to treat each function as a separate indirect cost pool, to allocate each pool on a separate basis, and then to combine the separate allocations for inclusion on the summary cost allocation plan.

The Printing Division allocations may be handled by dividing the Printing Division's budget into the following three activities, with each included on a separate "costs to be allocated" schedule: central

Table 5.24 County Example: Central Service Cost Allocation Plan Printing Division: Central Office Supply Allocation of Costs for Fiscal Year Ended June 30, 1979

	Number of Central Stores Tickets[a]	Percent	Allocation
Commissioner of revenue	19	9.77	$ 1,489
Real estate assessments	51	6.30	960
Treasurer	87	10.75	1,638
Electoral board	43	5.32	811
Police	68	8.41	1,281
Fire	34	4.20	640
Inspections	29	3.58	545
Utilities-solid waste	15	1.85	282
Transportation	46	5.69	867
Human resources	33	4.08	622
Libraries	42	5.19	791
Environmental affairs	43	5.32	811
Utilities	31	3.83	584
Social services	29	3.58	545
County board	14	1.73	264
County manager	27	3.34	509
Fiscal analysis	29	3.58	545
Personnel	34	4.20	640
Other agencies	75	9.28	1,413
Total to be allocated	809	100.00	$15,237[b]
Other central services	89		
Grand total	898		

[a] Based on a sample of central stores "tickets" by agency.
[b] Excludes supply costs billed to agencies.

143

**Table 5.25 County Example: Central Service Cost
Allocation Plan Printing Division: Mail Room
Allocation of Costs for Fiscal Year Ended
June 30, 1979**

	Direct-Billed Metered Postage	Percent	Allocation
Commissioner of revenue	$ 32,186	20.02	$ 4,029
Real estate assessments	5,678	3.53	710
Treasurer	41,517	25.82	5,196
Electoral board	2,655	1.65	332
Police	5,927	3.69	743
Fire	848	0.53	107
Inspections	1,671	1.04	209
Utilities-solid waste	1,948	1.21	244
Transportation	290	0.18	36
Human resources	834	0.52	105
Libraries	8,874	5.52	1,111
Environmental affairs	8,665	5.39	1,085
Utilities	25,339	15.76	3,172
Social services	14,500	9.02	1,815
County board	1,216	0.76	153
County manager	74	0.05	10
Fiscal analysis	1,704	1.06	213
Personnel	3,396	2.11	424
Other agencies	3,443	2.14	430
Total to be allocated	$160,765	100.00	$20,124[a]
Other central service agencies	1,202		
Grand total	$161,967		

[a] Excludes postage billed directly to agencies.

Table 5.26 County Example: Central Service Cost Allocation Plan Printing Division: Printing and Duplicating Allocation of Costs for Fiscal Year Ended June 30, 1979

	Direct-Billed Duplication/ Printing Costs	Percent	Allocation
Commissioner of revenue	$ 5,001	1.70	$ 2,379
Real estate assessments	4,236	1.44	2,015
Treasurer	3,892	1.32	1,847
Electoral board	1,792	0.61	854
Police	24,396	8.29	11,601
Fire	3,562	1.21	1,693
Inspections	10,932	3.71	5,192
Utilities-solid waste	1,876	0.64	896
Transportation	9,571	3.25	4,548
Human resources	8,941	3.04	4,254
Libraries	13,442	4.57	6,395
Environmental affairs	45,118	15.33	21,452
Utilities	5,434	1.85	2,589
Social services	12,748	4.33	6,059
County board	11,833	4.02	5,625
County manager	41,038	13.94	19,507
Fiscal analysis	8,433	2.86	4,002
Personnel	19,612	6.66	9,320
Other agencies	62,479	21.23	29,708
Total to be allocated	$294,336	100.00	$139,936[a]
Other central service agencies	10,736		
	$305,072		

[a] Duplication and printing costs billed to user agencies are excluded from this total on "costs to be allocated" schedules.

Table 5.27 County Example: Central Service Cost Allocation Plan
Printing Division Allocation of Costs Summary
for Fiscal Year Ended June 30, 1979

	Table 5.24 Central Office Stores	Table 5.25 Mail Room	Table 5.26 Printing and Duplicating	Total Costs Allocated for Printing Division
Commissioner of revenue	$ 1,489	$ 4,029	$ 2,379	$ 7,897
Real estate assessments	960	710	2,015	3,685
Treasurer	1,638	5,196	1,847	8,681
Electoral board	811	332	854	1,997
Police	1,281	743	11,601	13,625
Fire	640	107	1,693	2,440
Inspections	545	209	5,192	5,946
Utilities-solid waste	282	244	896	1,422
Transportation	867	36	4,548	5,451
Human resources	622	105	4,254	4,981
Libraries	791	1,111	6,395	8,297
Environmental affairs	811	1,085	21,452	23,348
Utilities	584	3,172	2,589	6,345
Social services	545	1,815	6,059	8,419
County board	264	153	5,625	6,042
County manager	509	10	19,507	20,026
Fiscal analysis	545	213	4,002	4,760
Personnel	640	424	9,320	10,384
Other agencies	1,413	430	29,708	31,551
Total	$ 15,237	$ 20,124	$139,936	$175,297

office supply, mail room, and printing and duplicating, the largest activity. On the "costs to be allocated" schedule for each of these, any direct-billed charges made to users should be deducted. The example cost allocations for the activities are shown in Tables 5.24–5.26, with a separate allocation basis used for each. As a final step, the costs allocated on the three schedules are combined on Table 5.27.

Case C. Costs Billed to User Agencies

This case of a central service agency that directly bills (charges) to users a portion of its costs has been discussed previously. It is being presented separately at this point to offer an alternate means of handling the direct-billed costs. The procedure recommended in Step 6 is to exclude the direct-billed costs from the "costs to be allocated" schedule and then to allocate only the balance of the agency's costs.

An alternative illustrated in Table 5.28 for a data processing operation is to subtract the direct charges on the "allocation of costs" schedule. This example shows in the first column the allocation basis—direct charges—and a "gross cost allocation" in the third column that includes billed and nonbilled costs. The

**Table 5.28 County Example: Central Service Cost Allocation Plan
Data Analysis and Processing Division (1.1032) Allocation
of Costs for Fiscal Year Ended June 30, 1977**

	Allocation Basis: Direct Charges to Users	Percent	Gross Cost Allocation	Less Charges to Users	Net Cost Allocation
Operating Department					
District Court—Alcohol Safety Action Program	$ 500	0.09	$ 814	$ 500	$ 314
Sheriff and jail	505	0.09	814	505	309
Commissioner of revenue	37,800	6.54	59,175	37,800	21,375
Real estate assessments	33,240	5.75	52,027	33,240	18,787
Treasurer	73,968	12.80	115,817	73,968	41,849
Electoral board	5,250	0.91	8,234	5,250	2,984
Police	64,260	11.12	100,616	64,260	36,356
Inspections	880	0.15	1,357	880	477
Utilities-solid waste	7,560	1.31	11,853	7,560	4,293
Transportation	600	0.10	905	600	305
Libraries	16,320	2.82	25,516	16,320	9,196
Environmental affairs	20,000	3.46	31,307	20,000	11,307
Social services	67,675	11.71	105,954	67,675	38,279
Utilities: water-sewer	63,000	10.90	98,625	63,000	35,625
Fiscal analysis	68,040	11.77	106,497	68,040	38,457
Personnel	99,750	17.26	156,172	99,750	56,422
Total county	$559,348	96.78	$875,683	$559,348	$316,335
Outside Agencies					
Retirement board	$ 5,000	.87	7,872	5,000	2,872
Credit union	6,000	1.04	9,410	6,000	3,410
Cigarette tax board	3,600	.62	5,610	3,600	2,010
City of Falls Church	4,000	.69	6,243	4,000	2,243
Total outside agencies	$ 18,600	3.22	$ 29,135	$ 18,600	$ 10,535
Total to be allocated	$577,948	100.00	$904,818	$577,948	$326,870
Central Service Agencies					
County manager	$ 1,260				
Printing division	2,243				
Automotive equipment	525				
Total central service agencies	$ 4,028				
Grand total	$581,976				

direct charges are then subtracted to yield the "net cost allocation" in the last column. In this case, where direct charges are the allocation basis, the subtraction of the costs as shown in Table 5.28 or the deletion of the costs on the "costs to be allocated" schedule makes no substantive difference. However, if another allocation basis is used, there may be a significant difference, and the method shown in Table 5.28 may be the preferred one to use.

Case D. CETA Grants

In the cost allocation process, Comprehensive Employment and Training Act (CETA) employees should be treated as locally funded employees are. That is, CETA employees should be included in the departments where they are assigned, and indirect costs allocated to departments would at the same time be allocated to the CETA program to the extent that the grant employees are assigned to those departments. Therefore, the CETA program should not affect the preparation of the cost allocation plan except in increasing cost allocations to the departments where the CETA employees work. However, the CETA program is treated differently in computing the indirect cost rates. This subject is discussed at the end of Chapter 6.

Schedule:	A-1	B-1	C-1	D-1	E-1	F-1
						Central

Operating Agency	City Manager's Office	Office of Management and Budget	Public Information	Community Relations	Personnel	Finance Department Accounting
Mayor and council	$ —	$ 470	$ 488	$ —	$ —	$ 859
Boards and commissions	—	39	40	—	—	71
City attorney	123	254	264	45	178	465
Fire	12,785	10,506	10,913	4,678	17,862	19,193
Police	12,908	13,106	13,613	4,723	18,032	23,941
Civil defense	—	55	57	—	—	101
Communications: operations and maintenance	3,135	2,638	2,740	1,147	4,379	4,818
Recorder's court	—	138	144	—	—	253
Public works	21,936	19,426	20,179	8,027	30,643	35,487
Parks and recreation	4,138	4,468	4,641	1,514	5,776	8,162
Community development and planning	2,882	3,423	3,555	1,055	4,032	6,253
General services: Airport	293	431	448	108	407	788
Finance: collection and city clerk	499	343	356	183	703	625
Subtotal[a]	$ 58,699	$ 55,297	$ 57,438	$ 21,480	$ 82,012	$101,016

Exhibit A
Cost Allocation Plan
Central Service Costs
June 30, 1978

G-1	H-1	I-1	J-1	K-1	L-1	
Service Agency						
Communications Telephone	General Services Garage	General Services Building Operations and Maintenance	General Services Purchasing	General Services Printing and Mail	Computer Services	Total
$ —	$ —	$ 4,750	$ —	$ —	$ —	$ 6,567
—	—	—	—	—	—	150
—	—	—	—	—	—	1,329
7,365	18,994	32,529	576	—	—	135,401
14,730	89,060	62,658	1,158	5,992	1,774	261,695
—	943	6,555	384	931	—	9,026
—	1,318	5,597	1,542	—	—	27,314
—	—	—	—	—	—	535
6,545	246,762	9,708	6,936	1,137	2,365	409,151
7,365	17,926	64,874	5,394	2,238	—	126,496
13,094	6,407	8,429	4,050	2,720	—	55,900
—	1,658	50,267	384	128	—	54,912
—	—	2,581	384	1,158	9,755	16,587
$ 49,099	$383,068	$247,948	$ 20,808	$ 14,304	$ 13,894	$1,105,063

Table 5.29 (Continued)

Schedule:	A-1	B-1	C-1	D-1	E-1	F-1 Central
Operating Agency	City Manager's Office	Office of Management and Budget	Public Information	Community Relations	Personnel	Finance Department Accounting
Allocation to other central service agencies	—	—	—	—	2,684	—
Total allocation[b]	$ 58,699	$ 55,297	$ 57,438	$ 21,480	$ 84,696	$101,016
Allocation from other central service agencies	(2,442)	—	(3,042)	—	(1,331)	(15,683)
Total central service costs[c]	$ 56,257	$ 55,297	$ 54,396	$ 21,480	$ 83,365	$ 85,333

[a] The "Subtotal" is the total allocation of central service agency costs to operating
[b] The "Total Allocation" is the total distribution of central service agency costs to
[c] The final total equals the "Total Allocation" less the allocations received by the

Exhibit A (Continued)

G-1 Service Agency	H-1	I-1	J-1	K-1	L-1	
Communi- cations Tele- phone	General Services Garage	General Services Building Opera- tions and Mainte- nance	General Services Purchas- ing	General Services Printing and Mail	Computer Services	Total
—	—	16,859	37,376	3,191	15,666	75,776
$ 49,099	$383,068	$264,807	$ 58,184	$17,495	$ 29,560	$1,180,839
—	(52,096)	(1,182)	—	—	—	(75,776)
$ 49,099	$330,972	$263,625	$ 58,184	$ 17,495	$ 29,560	$1,105,063

agencies only.
operating and other central service agencies.
central service agencies from other central service agencies.

Step 10. Summarize All Allocations to Operating Agencies

This final step of the plan preparation process requires construction of a summary of the "allocation of costs" schedules for all indirect cost pools. Tables 5.29 and 5.30 illustrate the summary process. The summary table is constructed by listing the following:

• Central service agencies are named across the top of the table.

• Operating agencies to which costs are allocated are placed down the left side of the table. Each operating agency to which costs are allocated in any "allocation of costs" schedule should be listed, although some operating agencies that do not operate federal grant programs may be summarized on one line.

After listing the agencies, the costs from each "allocation of costs" schedule may be entered in the appropriate column. For example, the costs from Table 5.30 for the Purchasing Division are entered in column J–1. The costs allocated to other central service agencies are entered on a separate line below the subtotal line. These costs will be discussed subsequently.

**Table 5.30 City Example: Central Service Cost Allocation
Plan General Services Department: Purchasing
(01–726–7082) Allocation of Costs for
Fiscal Year Ended June 30, 1978**

	Number of Requi- sitions[a]	Percent	Allocation
Fire	36	0.99	$ 576
Police	72	1.99	1,158
Civil defense	24	0.66	384
Communications	96	2.65	1,542
Public works	432	11.92	6,936
Parks and recreation	336	9.27	5,394
Community development and planning	252	6.96	4,050
Finance: Collection and city clerk	24	·0.66	384
General services: Airport	24	0.66	384
General services: Garage	2,328	64.24	37,376
Total to be allocated	3,624	100.00	$58,184[b]
Other Central Service Agencies[c]			
City manager	8		
Management and budget	27		
Public information	9		
Community relations	5		
Personnel	37		
Finance: Accounting	33		
General services: Building	43		
Computer services	4		
Subtotal other central service agencies	166		
Total requisitions	3,790		

[a] A sample of requisitions by agency is used as the allocation basis.
[b] Allocated from Table 5.19.
[c] Central service agencies other than the Garage are not burdened because of the relatively small number of requisitions they generate.

Summary of Costs

After costs are entered in each column, the preparer totals the costs appearing in each row to yield the indirect costs allocated to each operating agency. For example, the Police Department has had the following indirect costs allocated to it from central service agencies:

City Manager's Office	$ 12,908
Office of Management and Budget	13,106
Public Information	13,613
Community Relations	4,723
Personnel	18,032
Finance	23,941
Telephone	14,730
Garage	89,060
Building O and M	62,658
Purchasing	1,158
Printing and Mail	5,992
Computer Services	1,774
	$261,695

The total of $261,695 in indirect costs allocated to the Police Department is used in the following chapter to compute the indirect cost rate for the department.

Reconciliation of Totals

By completing the portion of the cost allocation plan below the subtotal line, the preparer is able to reconcile the allocation totals with the budget or financial report totals with which he began the allocation process. The reconciliation process is the following:

1 Each column is totaled to equal the subtotal—all costs allocated only to operating (not central service) agencies. For each central service agency this subtotal includes costs allocated from other central service agencies and excludes costs allocated to other central service agencies.

2 The allocations to other central service agencies are added back in to the appropriate columns. For example, in Table 5.29 the $37,376 shown in column J–1 represents the Purchasing Division costs allocated to the Garage, another central service agency.

3 The allocations received from other central service agencies are then deducted from the total allocation line. For each central service agency, the total equals the agency's operating budget less unallowable costs plus depreciation or use allowance costs, where applicable.

The preceding exercise of reconciliation is not required for the cost allocation process. However, it is recommended to assist the preparer in checking allocation totals.

6. Preparation of Departmental Indirect Cost Proposals

Completion of the 10 steps in the previous chapter yields a total amount of indirect costs allocated to each operating agency from all central service agencies. Preparation of the indirect cost proposal for an operating agency involves taking the indirect costs from the cost allocation plan, adding these costs to departmental indirect costs, and dividing this total by the salary and wage base for the operating department. As previously discussed, the multirate plan preparation method permits indirect costs within operating departments to be included in the indirect cost proposals. The procedure of preparing an indirect cost proposal requires these five steps that are described in this chapter:

1 Choose the method to be used for the indirect cost proposals.
2 List the direct and indirect cost areas to be included in the indirect cost proposal.
3 Identify the direct cost base for the department.
4 Identify the indirect costs within the operating department and from the cost allocation plan.
5 Total all direct and indirect costs and compute the indirect cost rate.

Step 1. Choose the Method to Be Used for the Indirect Cost Proposals

OASC–10 presents four alternate methods for preparing indirect cost proposals after a cost allocation plan has been completed. The four methods differ in two respects: (1) the level at which indirect costs are identified within the operating department and (2) whether individual rates are computed for each division or only one rate is computed for the department. Although the first method—the Short Form Method—is used as an example in the following pages, the other three methods are also described as possible options.

Short Form Method*

The Short Form Method illustrated in Appendix 9 and described in more detail later in this section involves preparing one rate for an individual department. It is assumed that no significant differences occur between the department's divisions in what levels of services they receive from the central service agencies. Also, only department-wide indirect costs are identified, such as the costs of a department director's office.

Simplified Method*

Under the Simplified Method, only one indirect cost rate is computed for the entire department, as with

* The Short Form Method and Simplified Method of indirect cost proposal preparation should not be confused with the method described in Chapter 4 of this guide for cost allocation plan preparation.

the Short Form Method. Again, the assumption is that each division's ratio of total indirect costs to direct costs is approximately the same as for all other divisions. The difference is that this method identifies indirect costs within divisions, as well as department-wide indirect costs. For example, costs of a division chief's office operation may be included in the indirect cost rate proposal. Therefore, within each division the preparer must separate direct from indirect costs. Appendix 10 shows the sample format presented in OASC–10 for this method.

Alternate Simplified Method

This alternative to the Simplified Method is identical to that method with one exception: a separate indirect cost rate is computed for each division. The preparer should use this method if he determines that the ratios of indirect to direct costs within divisions differ significantly. Therefore, the example shown in Appendix 11 states in Note b that the ratios among the divisions differ significantly and that a separate rate for each division is required. Under this method the costs from the central service cost allocation plan are allocated to the divisions in proportion to the direct salaries and wage costs in those divisions. (See Appendix 10, Note d.)

Multiple Rate Method

As with the Simplified and the Alternate Simplified methods, the Multiple Rate Method recognizes division-level indirect costs, as well as department-wide and central service agency indirect costs. Similar to the Alternate Simplified Method, a separate rate is computed for each division. The difference is that the central service costs allocated to the department from the cost allocation plan are allocated to divisions within the department on bases that reflect the levels of services received by the divisions. In addition, the department-wide indirect costs are allocated to the divisions on rational bases reflecting the levels of services received. As shown in Appendix 12, this method recognizes differing levels of supportive services received by the divisions and computes a separate rate indirect cost rate for each division.

Choice of Method

The examples used in this chapter assume that the preparer chooses the first method—the Short Form Method. Because each of the four methods requires a different procedure, the examples presented herein focus on this method for simplicity's sake. However,

Table 6.1 City Example: Indirect Cost Proosal: Police Department for Fiscal Year Ended June 30, 1978

Cost Areas	Total Costs	Unallowable Costs	Direct Costs Salaries and Wages / Other		Allowable Indirect Costs
	1	2	3	4	5
Direct Costs					
Jail					
Patrol					
Community relations					
Investigations					
Records					
Animal league					

164

School guards
Tactical squad
Crime prevention
Parking control
    Direct cost subtotal

Departmental Indirect Costs
Administration

***Central Service Cost
Allocation Plan Costs***
Exhibit A

    Total costs

      Rate calculation

the example formats shown in appendices 10, 11, and 12 should assist the preparer to use one of the other methods if he wishes.

Step 2. List the Direct and Indirect Cost Areas to Be Included in the Indirect Cost Proposal

Format for Proposal

Before listing the cost areas the preparer should construct the format for the indirect cost proposal. Table 6.1 is a modification of the format recommended in OASC–10 for the Simplified Method. (See Appendix 9.) Table 6.1 does not include the second column shown in Appendix 9—"excludable costs"—because this column would generally not pertain to local governments.

Three Cost Areas

Along the left side of Table 6.1 are listed the cost areas for a city police department, the example to be used here. Three major cost categories are included:

1 Direct costs of departmental divisions.

2 Indirect costs within the department.

3 Indirect costs from the central service cost allocation plan.

Under the first category are listed all divisions or budget/accounting units of the department—Jail, Patrol, Community Relations, and others. In the example's departmental indirect cost area, all the department-wide indirect costs are located in one budget unit—Administration. However, these costs might be included in several divisions or sections. In the Appendix 9 example, indirect cost areas listed are Office of the Director, Financial Management, Administrative Services, and Equipment Use.

Automotive Equipment Use Allowance

Chapter 5 includes the use allowance on automotive equipment used by the department in the central service cost allocation plan as part of the costs of the city garage operation. However, these costs may be included instead as indirect costs within the department and shown separately on the indirect cost rate proposal.

*Central Service Cost
Allocation Plan Costs*

Besides direct and indirect departmental costs, the third cost area in the proposal includes all costs allocated to the department through the central service cost allocation plan. Although the Appendix 9 example lists the indirect cost areas separately, Table 6.1 shows all costs on one line with reference given to "Exhibit A," the cost allocation plan.

Step 3. Identify the Direct Cost Base for the Department

This step requires listing the costs of all activities or divisions of the department other than those to be included as indirect cost areas. Columns 1–4 of Table 6.2 are completed as follows:

Column 1.
 Total Costs of the divisions are entered here.

Column 2.
 Unallowable costs entered in this column are the costs of capital items. (This column is meaningless for the direct cost areas, and these capital

costs may be moved to column 4, with no effect on the indirect cost rate.)

Column 3.

Salaries and wages are entered for the divisions. This column must include salaries for grant programs operated by the department, as well as locally funded salaries. If fringe benefits, as well as salaries and wages, are used as indirect cost base, the fringes should also be included.

Column 4.

Other costs not included in columns 2 and 3 are listed. Materials, supplies and contractual services should be included. Columns 2, 3, and 4 should equal column 1.

Step 4. Identify the Indirect Costs within the Operating Department and from the Cost Allocation Plan

The total costs of the divisions and sections providing department-wide supportive services are entered in column 1. Although Table 6.2 includes only one cost area, some jurisdictions may have several divisions or sections providing supportive services to the operating divisions. Costs within the department should be evaluated with the same scrutiny as the

Table 6.2 City Example: Indirect Cost Proposal: Police Department for Fiscal Year Ended June 30, 1978

Cost Areas	Total Costs	Unallowable Costs	Salaries and Wages	Other	Allowable Indirect Costs
	1	2	3	4	5
			Direct Costs		
Direct Costs					
Jail	$ 68,719		$ 15,598	$ 53,121	
Patrol	892,025	$40,300	647,952	203,773	
Community relations	53,122	800	39,706	12,616	
Investigations	316,116	15,200	239,064	61,852	
Records	129,802	800	103,251	25,751	
Animal league	18,850			18,850	
School guards	46,345		37,855	8,490	
Tactical squad	86,583	200	69,577	16,806	

Crime prevention	16,102	750	11,813	3,539	
Parking control	19,985		15,750	4,235	
Direct cost subtotal	$1,647,649	$58,050	$1,180,566	$409,033	

Departmental Indirect Costs

Administration	117,349	2,950	—	—	$114,399

Central Service Cost Allocation Plan Costs

Exhibit A (Table 5.29)	261,695				261,695
Total costs	$2,026,693	$61,000	$1,180,566	$409,033	$376,094

Rate calculation

$$\frac{\text{indirect costs (column 5)}}{\text{direct salaries and wages (column 3)}} = \frac{\$376,094}{\$1,180,566} = 0.3186 = 31.86\%$$

costs included in the cost allocation plan. Tables 4.2 and 4.3 should be used as guides for evaluating the allowability of departmental indirect costs. Column 2 of Table 6.2 lists the costs for equipment and other capital items unallowable as indirect costs. The balance of the costs from column 1 are entered in column 5—salaries, wages, fringe benefits, supplies, and other allowable indirect costs of the division. The total indirect costs allocated to the department through the cost allocation plan are entered in columns 1 and 5. The unallowable costs have already been deducted.

Step 5. Total All Direct and Indirect Costs and Compute the Indirect Cost Rate

This last step requires totaling the columns. The indirect cost total in column 5 is divided by column 3's direct salaries and wages to yield the indirect cost rate for the department. As shown at the bottom of Table 6.1, the $376,094 of indirect costs divided by the $1,180,566 of direct salaries and wages for the Police Department yields an indirect cost rate of 31.86%. This rate, after approval by the federal cognizant agency, may be applied to all grants operated by the Police Department. This same procedure is followed for each department that operates a federal grant program.

Grant Programs Crossing Department Lines

The preceding methodology pertains to grant programs located within individual departments. However, it may be necessary to compute separate rates for grant programs operated by two or more departments. OASC–10 does not discuss this problem; the solution offered in this guide must be approved by cognizant and grantor agencies.

The recommended solution is to compute a weighted average rate for the two or more departments operating the grant program. For example, if a law enforcement demonstration project were operated jointly by a probation office and a sheriff's department, a weighted average rate for the two departments could be computed, with the weighting factor being the total salaries of grant employees assigned to the respective departments.

For the computation shown, the following are "givens":

Department	Percent Indirect Cost Rates	Number of Grant Employees	Total Salaries Grant Employees
Sheriff	20.23	7	$ 72,100
Probation	15.19	2	19,800
Total		9	$ 91,900

The computation of the weighted average would proceed as follows:

	Rate ×	Grant Salaries =	Weighted Total
1. Sheriff	0.2023 ×	$72,100 =	$14,585.83
2. Probation	0.1519 ×	19,800 =	3,007.62
3. Weighted total			$17,593.45
4. ÷ Total salaries		÷	91,900
5. Weighted average indirect cost rate			0.1914

For this example the 19.14% weighted average between the two departments would apply to the total grant. In a situation where the grant program is jointly operated by two or more departments and no assignment may be made of employees to a specific department, a simple average of the dates among the departments may be considered.

Comprehensive Employment and Training Act (CETA)

Although the preceding methodology may be considered for CETA programs, it is possible that the large number of departments to which CETA employees are assigned will make the computation difficult to justify. An additional problem that arises is how to handle employees assigned to central service agencies, for which indirect cost rates are not computed. In the preparation of indirect cost proposals, the CETA program is considered a special case, not only because employees work in several departments, but also because the CETA regulations severely limit the types and amounts of indirect costs that may be charged to this federal program.

First, the regulations prohibit the use of CETA funds for "normal" local government functions, as described in the following section:

§ 676.40   Allowable costs.

(a) *General.* To be allowable, a cost must be necessary and reasonable for proper and efficient administration of the program, be allocable thereto under these principles, and, except as specifically provided herein, not be an expense normally incurred to carry out the responsibilities of State or local government in the absence of funds under the Act.*

In addition, the CETA regulations prohibit funds to be used to supplant existing local funds, as noted in this section:

§ 676.73   Maintenance of effort.

(a) To ensure maintenance of effort under all programs under the Act

* *Federal Register,* April 3, 1979, p. 20022.

(b) Funds under this Act shall supplement, and not supplant, the level of funds that would otherwise be made available from non-Federal sources for the planning and administration of programs (sec. 121(g)(1)(c)).*

This guide recommends that the preparer seek the advice of the Department of Labor's regional negotiator regarding how the regulations will be applied to the indirect cost proposals. See Appendix 1.

* *Federal Register,* April 3, 1979, p. 20029.

7. Summary: Contents of Final Submission

This chapter summarizes the items contained in a jurisdiction's indirect cost plan package. The first section outlines the elements of the submission for the short form method described in Chapter 4; the second section outlines the elements of the long form method described in Chapters 5 and 6. Along with the items listed in this chapter, a copy of the jurisdiction's adopted budget or audited financial report should be available for review by the cognizant federal agency. Also, copies of all working papers should be retained for a possible audit of the plan.

As discussed previously, an outside auditor should be able to trace every number contained in the cost allocation plan and indirect cost proposals back to a budget, audit, or working papers.

CONTENTS OF SHORT FORM PLAN

Consolidated Cost Allocation Plan
and Indirect Cost Proposal

As illustrated in Table 4.1, the consolidated plan usually comprises one page and has three parts:

1 Identification of all indirect costs (indirect cost pool).
2 Identification of all other costs of the local government.
3 Computation of the indirect cost rate.

The allocation plan is, in short, a restatement of the jurisdiction's budget or financial report, with allowable indirect costs identified separately from other costs.

Certification of Plan

The chief executive or other designated official certifies that the plan was prepared in accordance with the federal policies and procedures outlined in Federal Guide OASC–10 and Federal Management Circular 74–4 (also contained in OASC–10). The prescribed certification form is shown as Table 7.1. The third box should be checked for the short form plan described in Chapter 4.

Federal Funds Schedule

This item is a listing of federal funds received or to be received by the jurisdiction. For each federal agency, this breakdown of costs should be included: salaries and wages, other costs, and total costs. If the audited financial report is the basis for the plan, then actual expenditures should be included in this schedule; if the budget is the basis, then those figures should be shown. An example schedule is shown as Table 7.2.

Schedule of Inconsistently Handled Cost Areas

This schedule lists the indirect cost areas handled inconsistently among federal grant programs or be-

Table 7.1 Sample Form: Certification by an Agency Government Official.

I hereby certify that the information contained in the

Check One:

☐ Indirect Cost Proposal
☐ Central Service Cost Allocation Plan
☐ Consolidated Central Service Cost Allocation Plan/Indirect Cost Proposal

for the fiscal year ended _____ and which is attached to this certification is
(Month-date-year)
prepared in conformance with Federal Management Circular 74-4 and the implementing instructions contained in the Guide OASC-10 published by the department of Health, Education, and Welfare. I further certify: (1) that no costs other than those incurred by the grantee/contractor or allocated to the grantee/contractor via an approved central service cost allocation plan were included in its indirect cost pool as finally accepted, and that such incurred costs are legal obligations of the grantee/contractor and allowable under the governing cost principles, (2) that the same costs that have been treated as indirect costs have not been claimed as direct costs, (3) that similar types of costs have been accorded consistent accounting treatment, and (4) that the information provided by the grantee/contractor which was used as a basis for acceptance of the rate(s) agreed to herein is not subsequently found to be materially inaccurate.

_____
Signature

_____
Name

_____
Title

_____
Name of State or Local Government

_____
Name of Dept. or Agency (for indirect cost proposal only)

_____
Date

Table 7.2 Schedule of Federal Fund Expenditures

Source	Direct Salaries and Wages	Other Direct Expenditures	Total Expenditures
Department of Justice: Law Enforcement Assistance Administration	$ 11,693.00	$ 69,517.00	$ 81,210.00
Department of Labor: CETA	398,271.27	65,007.15	463,278.42
Civil Service Commission:			
Intergovernmental Personnel Act		3,659.82	3,659.82
National Endowment for the Humanities		4,679.88	4,679.88
Department of the Interior		55,846.00	55,846.00
Department of Housing and Urban Development: Community Development	210,962.97	1,369,786.71	1,580,749.68
Department of the Treasury: Revenue Sharing	613,257.36	1,051,804.66	1,665,062.02
Department of the Treasury: Anti-Recession		163,910.82	163,910.82
Department of Transportation: Federal Highway Safety Grant	5,034.96	895.26	5,930.22
Total	$1,239,219.56	$2,785,107.30	$4,024,326.86

tween federal grant programs and nonfederal programs. The inconsistency is in the treatment of cost items as indirect costs for one program and as direct costs for another. An example is a rental fee for city-owned vehicles that the city charges to a federal grant, but does not charge to other city agencies. Such inconsistent treatment may be acceptable to cognizant agency officials if the jurisdiction can show that the federal grant program is being charged a fair amount in relation to the costs of providing the service. The jurisdiction should be able to show that had other local agencies been charged for the same services as the federal grant programs, those amounts would have been proportionately the same as the federal grant charges. The jurisdiction would perform a "memorandum billing" to all agencies. See OASC–10, p. 9 (#4), for a more detailed explanation of this schedule.

Organizational Chart and
Statement of Functions

This chart should show the entire organizational structure of the local government. No particular form is required by OASC–10. Also, a statement of the functions of all activities of the governmental unit is required. Local staff should find out from the cognizant agency what degree of detail is required in this statement, because the organizational chart may provide a sufficient explanation.

CONTENTS OF LONG FORM PLAN

This section describes each element of the long form plan and reviews the basic contents of each. The four items in Part 1 are identical to elements of the short form plan. The reader should refer back to the explanations of these elements provided earlier.

Part 1—General

- Certification by local government official.

- Organizational chart.

- Federal funds schedule.

- Schedule of inconsistently handled cost areas.

Part 2—Central Service Cost Allocation Plan

Summary of Allocated Central Service Costs

As described in Step 10 of Chapter 5, through this table summarizes all "allocation of costs" schedules for the central service agencies. Each column of the summary schedule shown on Table 5.29 comprises one "allocation of costs" schedule.

Summary of Central Services
Billed to User Agencies

This summary, illustrated in Table 5.7, describes the jurisdiction's central services charged or billed to user agencies. Along with a definition of what services are charged is an explanation of the bases for the charges.

Allocation of Costs Schedule

For each central service agency the cost allocation plan should include an "allocation of costs" schedule that has the data used as the allocation basis, the percentage of distribution among user agencies of the allocation units, and the allocation of all allowable costs. Tables 5.17 and 5.18 illustrate the allocation schedule.

Costs to be Allocated Schedule

The preparer includes for each central service agency a "costs to be allocated" schedule that includes: the total budget (or actual expenditures) for the central service agency, deductions of unallowable costs such as capital and federal funds, and additions of costs allocated to the agency from other central service agencies. See Tables 5.8 and 5.9 as examples.

Statement of Function and Benefit

This schedule explains the services provided by a central service agency and highlights the benefits provided to grant programs. In addition, the schedule includes an explanation of the allocation basis used for the distribution of the agency's costs and the rationale for using that basis. A sample statement of function and benefit schedule is shown in Table 5.5.

Part 3—Indirect Cost Proposals for Operating Agencies

The indirect cost proposal, explained in Chapter 6, includes the direct and indirect costs within the agency, the indirect costs from the cost allocation plan, and the computation of the agency's indirect cost rate. As discussed in Chapter 2, only the indirect cost proposals for departments operating the grant programs funded by the cognizant agency should be submitted to the cognizant agency. Other indirect cost proposals should be submitted to the appropriate federal funding agency.

CONCLUSION: SOURCES OF ADDITIONAL HELP

An assumption I have held in writing this guide is that the process of preparing indirect cost plans need not be a deep, dark secret. Plan preparation may be a time-consuming process, but local government finance officials are capable of understanding the process and of preparing plans for their own jurisdictions, given adequate time. Also, despite the large time investment required to prepare and negotiate the jurisdiction's first plan, succeeding plans are usually easier to prepare.

If a local government determines, however, that its staff cannot be freed from other duties to prepare a plan, many accounting and consulting firms have the staff capability to prepare and negotiate plans for local governments. In addition to the firms that frequently audit local government records, there are firms specializing in indirect cost plan preparation. If a firm is to be sought, a jurisdiction should consider issuing a request for proposal, because the fees for preparing plans may vary greatly from one firm to the next. In such a request for proposal, the locality should specify whether a single or multirate plan is desired and how much work the firm is expected to do in collecting financial and allocation basis data.

At this writing few workshops are available to local governments on this subject. Therefore, local officials should inform universities, state agencies, and professional organizations of their need for assistance in this area. For example, my organization, the University of South Carolina's Bureau of Governmental Research, has been very successful in assisting South Carolina local governments through workshops to prepare indirect cost plans.

Appendix 1. Excerpts from CETA Regulations

§ 676.40 Allowable costs.

(a) *General*. To be allowable, a cost must be necessary and reasonable for proper and efficient administration of the program, be allocable thereto under these principles, and, except as specifically provided herein, not be an expense normally incurred to carry out the responsibilities of State or local government in the absence of funds under the Act.

(b) *Direct costs*. Direct costs are those that can be identified specifically with a particular cost objective. These costs may be charged directly to grants, contracts or to other programs against which costs are finally lodged. Direct costs may also be charged to cost objectives used for the accumulation of costs pending distribution in due course to grants and other ultimate cost objectives.

(c) *Indirect costs.* (1) Indirect costs are those:

(i) Incurred for a common or joint purpose benefiting more than one cost objective; and

(ii) Not readily assignable to the cost objectives specifically benefited, without effort disproportionate to the results achieved. The term "indirect costs," as used herein, applies to costs of this type originating in the recipient entity, as well as those incurred by other entities in supplying goods, services, and facilities, to the recipient.

(2) Only the indirect cost rate approved by the cognizant Federal agency may be used by the recipient in determining indirect costs properly chargeable to CETA. The cognizant Federal agency is the Federal agency designated to determine the indirect cost rate or rates on behalf of all Federal agencies which award financial assistance to the recipient.

(d) *Restrictions on use of funds.* (1) The amount of funds available for any specific cost category or activity shall be limited as specified in the regulations for the specific programs.

(2) Funds made available through one grant or Annual Plan subpart may not be used to support costs properly chargeable to another grant or Annual Plan subpart with the exception that funds available for administration shall be pooled under a separate subpart and used to cover all allowable administrative costs incurred under the Annual Plan (sec. 123(f)).

§ 676.40–2   Administration and travel costs.

(a) The administrative cost contribution shall not exceed 20 percent of the total allocation for each Annual Plan Subpart other than Title II D, Title VI, the Youth Community

Conservation and Improvement Projects and the Special Governor's Grant unless the Program Narrative Description set forth an explanation of how all administrative costs have been determined and a detailed documentation to support that amount. The restriction on the contribution of funds to the Administrative Annual Plan Subpart for Title II D and Title VI programs is set forth in § 677.58(a) and § 678.8-(b)(1)(iii). The restriction on the contribution of administrative funds in the Youth Community Conservation and Improvement Projects is set forth in Part 680. Administrative cost contribution limitations for Title VII programs are found in Part 679 and for Special Governor's Grant programs in Part 677 Subpart D.

(b) No funds made available for administrative costs under any Title of the Act may be used by a prime sponsor for legal or other associated services from contractors unless the prime sponsor certifies in writing that:

(1) The payments are not unreasonable in relation to the fees charged by other contractors providing similar services; and

(2) The services could not be competently provided through employees of the prime sponsor or other available State or local governmental employees (sec. 123(f)(2)).

(c) The cost of participant travel and staff travel necessary for the operation or administration of programs under the Act is allowed as provided herein:

(1) Travel costs of governmental officials not part of the Office of the Governor of a State or the Chief executive of a political subdivision are allowable if costs specifically relate to programs under the Act. These costs shall be charged to administration.

(2) Travel costs for CETA administrative staff, including

participants in administrative positions, are allowable when the travel is specifically related to the operation of programs under the Act.

(3) Travel costs for participants using their personal automobiles in the performance of their jobs are allowable if the employing agency normally reimbursed its other employees in this manner. Such costs shall be charged to fringe benefits.

Source. Federal Register, April 3, 1979, pp. 20022 and 20023.

Appendix 2. Excerpts from Community Development Block Grant Regulations

Subpart C—Eligible Activities

§ 570.200   Eligible activities.

(a) Grant assistance for a Community Development Program may be used only for the following activities:

(13) Payment of reasonable administrative costs and carrying charges related to the planning and execution of community development and housing activities, including but not limited to (i) housing counseling and other activities designed to further the fair housing provisions of § 570.303(e)(1) and the housing objectives of § 570.303(c)(4)(ii), and (ii) the provision of information and, at the discretion of the recipient, of resources to residents of areas in which other community development activities described in § 570.303(b)

and the housing activities covered in the Housing Assistance Plan described in § 570.303(c) are to be concentrated with respect to the planning and execution of such activities.

(c) Costs incurred in carrying out the program, whether charged to the program on a direct or an indirect basis, must be in conformance with the requirements of Federal Management Circular 74-4, "Cost Principles Applicable to Grants and Contracts with State and Local Governments." All items of cost listed in Attachment B, Section C of that Circular (except Item 6, preagreement costs, which are eligible only to the extent authorized in § 570.302) are allowable without prior approval to the extent they constitute reasonable costs and are otherwise eligible under this Subpart.

[41 FR 2766, Jan. 19, 1976, as amended at 41 FR 20524, May 18, 1976; 41 FR 36899, Sept. 1, 1976, 41 FR 43887, Oct. 4, 1976]

§ 570.201 Ineligible activities.

Any type of activity not described in § 570.200 is ineligible. The following list of examples of ineligible activities is merely illustrative, and does not constitute a list of all ineligible activities.

(d) *General government expenses.* Except for the provisions of § 570.200(c), expenses required to carry out the regular responsibilities of the unit of general local government are not eligible. Examples include all ordinary general government expenditures not related to the community development program described pursuant to § 570.303(b) and not related to activities eligible under § 570.200.

Source. Code of Federal Regulations, Title 24-Housing and Urban Development, Part 570-Community Development Block Grants.

Appendix 3. Addresses of Federal Offices Regarding Circular 74-4

Source. OASC–10, pp. 84–88.

SECTION VI–ADDRESSES OF FEDERAL OFFICES TO
CONTACT REGARDING THE REQUIREMENTS OF CIRCULAR 74-4

Each Federal agency responsible for auditing and approving cost allocation plans, indirect cost proposals and other cost center proposals prepared by States and localities under Circular 74-4 has designated an office or offices which will carry out that responsibility. The offices and addresses for each agency are:

Community Services Administration
Office of the Controller
Community Services Administration
1200-19th Street, N.W., Room 324
Washington, D.C. 20506

Department of Agriculture
Director, Office of Management & Finance
U.S. Department of Agriculture
Room 102A, Administration Bldg.
14th and Independence Avenue, S.W.
Washington, D.C. 20250

Department of Commerce
Director
Office of Audits
U.S. Department of Commerce
14th and Constitution Avenue, N.W.
Washington, D.C. 20230

Department of Defense
Defense Civil Preparedness Agency COMP/AUD
Department of Defense, 1055 CWB
The Pentagon
Washington, D.C. 20301

Department of Health, Education, and Welfare

Assistant Regional Directors for Financial Management—Address

For State & Local Agencies In:

Region I:

John Fitzgerald Kennedy Federal Bldg.
Government Center
Boston, Massachusetts 02203

Connecticut, Maine, Massachusetts, New Hampshire, Rhode Island, Vermont

Region II:

Federal Office Bldg.
26 Federal Plaza
New York, New York 10007

New Jersey, New York, Puerto Rico

Region III:

Gateway Building
3535 Market Street
P.O. Box 13716
Philadelphia, Pennsylvania 19101

Delaware, Maryland, Pennsylvania, Washington, D.C., West Virginia, Virginia

Region IV:

Peachtree-Seventh Bldg.
50-7th Street, N.E.
Atlanta, Georgia 30323

Alabama, Florida, Georgia, Kentucky, Mississippi, North Carolina, South Carolina, Tennessee

ADDRESSES OF FEDERAL OFFICES, CIRCULAR 74–4

Department of Health, Education, and Welfare (Continued)

Assistant Regional Directors for Financial Management — Address	*For State & Local Agencies In:*
Region V:	
300 S. Wacker Drive Chicago, Illinois 60606	Illinois, Indiana, Michigan, Minnesota, Ohio, Wisconsin
Region VI:	
1200 Main Tower Dallas, Texas 75202	Arkansas, Louisiana, New Mexico, Oklahoma, Texas
Region VII:	
Federal Office Bldg. 601 East 12th Street Kansas City, Missouri 64106	Iowa, Kansas, Missouri, Nebraska
Region VIII:	
Federal Office Bldg. 1961 Stout Street Denver, Colorado 80202	Colorado, Montana, North Dakota, South Dakota, Utah, Wyoming
Region IX:	
Federal Office Bldg. 50 Fulton Street San Francisco, California 94102	Arizona, California, Hawaii, Nevada
Region X:	
Arcade Building, 1321 Second Avenue Seattle, Washington 98101	Alaska, Idaho, Oregon, Washington

Department of Housing and Urban Development*
Attn: Regional Administrator
    HUD Regional Office

Region I:

John F. Kennedy Federal Bldg.
Room 405
Boston, Massachusetts 02203

Region II:

26 Federal Plaza
New York, New York 10007

Region III:

Curtis Building
6th and Walnut Streets
Philadelphia, Pennsylvania 19106

Region IV:

211 Pershing Point Plaza
1371 Peachtree Street, N.E.
Atlanta, Georgia 30309

Region V:

300 South Wacker Drive
Chicago, Illinois 60606

Region VI:

New Dallas Federal Bldg.
1100 Commerce Street
Dallas, Texas 75202

Region VII:

Federal Office Bldg., Rm. 300
911 Walnut Street
Kansas City, Missouri 64106

Region VIII:

Federal Building
1961 Stout Street
Denver, Colorado 80202

Region IX:

450 Golden Gate Avenue
P.O. Box 36003
San Francisco, California 94102

Region X:

Arcade Plaza Bldg.
Room 226
Seattle, Washington 98101

---

*The States assigned to the HUD regional offices are the same as the Department of Health, Education & Welfare.

ADDRESSES OF FEDERAL OFFICES, CIRCULAR 74–4

Department of Interior
Eastern Regional Audit Manager
Office of Audit and Investigation
Department of Interior, Ballston Towers #1
801 N. Arlington Street, Room 401
Arlington, Virginia 22217

Central Regional Audit Manager
Office of Audit and Investigation
Department of the Interior
1841 Wadsworth
Lakewood, Colorado 80215

Western Regional Audit Manager
Office of Audit and Investigation
Department of Interior
Federal Office Building, Room W2219
2800 Cottage Way
Sacramento, California 95825

Department of Justice
Director, Office of Management and Finance
Internal Audit Staff
Department of Justice
Chester Arthur Bldg., Room 5031
425 I Street, N.W.
Washington, D.C. 20530

Department of Labor*

Regions I and II

Regional Administrator for Audit
U.S. Department of Labor, OASAM
1515 Broadway - Room 3505
New York, New York 10036

Attn: Regional Cost Negotiator .

Region III

Assistant Director, DA&I
Office of Cost Determination
U.S. Department of Labor, OASAM
200 Constitution Ave., N.W., Room S 5030
Washington, D.C. 20210

Regions VI, VII and VIII

Regional Administrator for Audit
U.S. Department of Labor, OASAM
555 Griffin Square - Room 205
Griffin and Young Streets
Dallas, Texas 75202

Attn: Regional Cost Negotiator

Region IV

Regional Administrator for Audit
U.S. Department of Labor, OASAM
1371 Peachtree Street, N.E., Room 240
Atlanta, Georgia 30309

Attn: Regional Cost Negotiator

Region V

Regional Administrator for Audit
U.S. Department of Labor, OASAM
Federal Office Bldg., Room 960
230 S. Dearborn Street
Chicago, Illinois 60604

Attn: Regional Cost Negotiator

Regions IX and X

Regional Administrator for Audit
U.S. Department of Labor, OASAM
450 Golden Gate Ave., Rm. 9403
San Francisco, California 94102

Attn: Regional Cost Negotiator

---

*The states assigned to the Dept. of Labor regional offices are the same as the Dept. of Health, Education & Welfare

Department of Transportation
Office of Installation and Logistics
TAD-60
Department of Transportation
400 7th Street, S.W.
Washington, D.C. 20590

Environmental Protection Agency
Chief, Cost Policy & Review Branch, (PM-214C)
Environmental Protection Agency
Room 711
Crystal Mall #2
Washington, D.C. 20460

Law Enforcement Assistance Administration
Comptroller
Law Enforcement Assistance Administration
Department of Justice
633 Indiana Avenue, N.W., Room 942
Washington, D.C. 20530

National Foundation on the Arts and the Humanities
Audit Supervisor
National Foundation on the Arts & the Humanities
806-15th Street, N.W., Room 516
Washington, D.C. 20506
Mail Stop 201

National Science Foundation
Audit Officer
National Science Foundation
1800 G Street, N.W., Room 245
Washington, D.C. 20550

Veterans Administration
Assistant Director for Accounting Systems (047D)
Finance Service
Office of Controller
Veterans Administration
810 Vermont Avenue, N.W.
Washington, D.C. 20420

U. S. GOVERNMENT PRINTING OFFICE : 1977 O - 250-671

199

Appendix 4. State and Local Department Unit Indirect Cost Negotiation Agreement

Source. OASC–10, pp. 73–76.

Indirect Cost Negotiation Agreement

SAMPLE FORMAT

STATE AND LOCAL DEPARTMENT UNIT
INDIRECT COST NEGOTIATION AGREEMENT

DATE: June 24, 1976

Department/Unit and
   State/Locality: (Insert Name and Address)

FILING REF.:   This replaces
Negotiation Agreement
dated   June 3, 1975

The indirect cost rate(s) contained herein is for use on grants and contracts with the Federal Government to which Federal Management Circular 74-4 applies subject to the limitations contained in Section II, A. of this agreement. The rate(s) was negotiated by the (insert the above named State or local department/agency) and the Department of (insert name of the Federal cognizant agency) in accordance with the authority contained in Attachment A, Section J.3. of the Circular.

SECTION I: Rates

Type	Effective Period From	To	Rate*	Locations	Applicable To
Final	7/1/74	6/30/75	10.65%	All	All Programs
Fixed	7/1/75	6/30/76	10.47%	All	All Programs
Fixed	7/1/76	6/30/77	10.28%	All	All Programs

*Base: Total direct salaries and wages.

Treatment of Fringe Benefits: Fringe benefits applicable to direct salaries and wages are treated as direct costs.

INDIRECT COST NEGOTIATION AGREEMENT

SECTION II: General

A. LIMITATIONS: Use of the rate(s) contained in this agreement is subject to any statutory or administrative limitations and is applicable to a given grant or contract only to the extent that funds are available. Acceptance of the rate(s) agreed to herein is predicated upon the conditions: (1) that no costs other than those incurred by the grantee/contractor or allocated to the grantee/contractor via an approved Central Service cost allocation plan were included in its indirect cost pool as finally accepted and that such incurred costs are legal obligations of the grantee/contractor and allowable under the governing cost principles, (2) that the same costs that have been treated as indirect costs have not been claimed as direct costs, (3) that similar types of costs have been accorded consistent treatment, and (4) that the information provided by the grantee/contractor which was used as a basis for acceptance of the rate(s) agreed to herein is not subsequently found to be materially inaccurate.

B. AUDIT: Adjustments to amounts resulting from audit of the cost allocation plan upon which the negotiation of this agreement was based will be compensated for in a subsequent negotiation.

C. CHANGES: If a fixed or predetermined rate(s) is contained in this agreement it is based on the organizational structure and the accounting system in effect at the time the proposal was submitted. Changes in the organizational structure or changes in the method of accounting for costs which affect the amount of reimbursement resulting from use of the rate(s) in this agreement, require the prior approval of the authorized representative of the responsible negotiation agency. Failure to obtain such approval may result in subsequent audit disallowances.

D. FIXED RATE(S): The fixed rate(s) contained in this agreement is based on an estimate of the costs which will be incurred during the period for which the rate applies. When the actual costs for such period have been determined, an adjustment will be made in the negotiation following such determination to compensate for the difference between that cost used to establish the fixed rate and that which would have been used were the actual costs known at the time.

E. NOTIFICATION TO FEDERAL AGENCIES: Copies of this document may be provided to other Federal offices as a means of notifying them of the agreement contained herein.

F. SPECIAL REMARKS: Federal programs currently reimbursing indirect costs to this Department/Agency by means other than the rate(s) cited in this agreement should be credited for such costs and the applicable rate cited herein applied to the appropriate base to identify the proper amount of indirect costs allocable to the program.

By the State or Local Department/Agency

Benjamin B. Knight _____ /s/

Benjamin B. Knight _____
Name

Director of Fiscal Affairs _____
Title

July 6, 1976 _____
Date

By the Responsible Agency for the Federal Government

Department of Health, Education, & Welfare _____
Agency

Truman P. Burrus _____ /s/

Truman P. Burrus _____
Name

Asst. Reg. Director for Fin. Mgmt. _____
Title

Date_____ July 15, 1976 _____

Negotiated by_____ Harry D. Giles _____

Telephone _____

202

Indirect Cost Negotiation Agreement

NEGOTIATION AGREEMENT
CENTRAL SERVICE COST ALLOCATIONS

DATE____March 15, 1976

STATE/LOCALITY: (Insert name and address)

FILING REF.:   This replaces
Negotiation Agreement
dated____February 26, 1975

Pursuant to Federal Management Circular 74-4, the Department of Health, Education, and Welfare approves the central service costs cited in this agreement. This approval is subject to the conditions contained in Section III.

SECTION I: Costs Distributed Through Central Service Cost Allocation Plan

---

The central service costs listed in Exhibit A, attached, are approved on a fixed with carry-forward basis for the fiscal year ending June 30, 1977 and may be included as part of the costs of the departments/agencies indicated in Exhibit A for further allocation to Federal grants and contracts performed by the respective departments/agencies.

SECTION II: Costs Distributed Through Billing Mechanisms

In addition to the costs distributed through cost allocations cited in Section I, the costs of the general services listed below may be billed to user departments/agencies:

Office of General Services

1. Automatic Data Processing
2. Reproduction
3. Communication

Motor Pool

1. Automobiles
2. Buses
3. Trucks

Charges for the above services shall be billed in accordance with rates established by the State/locality as described in its Central Service Cost Allocation Plan. Department/agency indirect cost rate proposals must clearly identify those costs that have been distributed through billing mechanisms as-well-as costs included in Section I of this Agreement.

203

INDIRECT COST NEGOTIATION AGREEMENT

SECTION III

A. LIMITATIONS: Use of the amounts contained in this agreement are subject to any statutory or administrative limitations and when ultimately allocated to individual grants or contracts through the indirect cost rates of each State/local department/agency, are applicable only to the extent that funds are available. Acceptance of the amounts agreed to herein is predicated on the conditions: (1) that no costs other than those incurred by the State/locality were included for distribution in its State/local-wide cost allocation plan as finally accepted and that such costs are legal obligations of the State/locality and allowable under the governing cost principles, (2) that similar types of costs have been accorded consistent accounting treatment, (3) that the information provided by the State/locality which was used as the basis for acceptance of the amounts or rates agreed to herein is not subsequently found to be materially incomplete or inaccurate.

B. CHANGES: If fixed or predetermined amounts are contained in this agreement, they are based on the organizational structure and the accounting system in effect at the time the plan was prepared and the agreement was negotiated. These amounts are subject to modification if changes are made in the organizational structure or in the method of accounting for costs which affect the amount of reimbursement resulting from use of the amounts. The authorized representative of the responsible negotiation agency must be notified of such changes prior to their effective date. Failure to provide this notification may result in subsequent cost disallowances.

C. FIXED AMOUNTS: If fixed amounts are contained in this agreement, they are based on an estimate of the costs that will be incurred during the period to which the amounts apply. When the actual costs for such period are determined, adjustments will be made in a subsequent negotiation to compensate for the differences between the costs used to establish the fixed amounts and the actual costs.

D. BILLED COSTS: Charges for the services cited in Section II will be billed in accordance with rates established by the State/Locality and recorded on the books of the operating department/agency responsible for providing the services. Such charges will be based on the actual, allowable costs, as defined in FMC 74-4, incurred by the operating department/agency responsible for providing the services. Variances resulting from differences between billed allowable costs and the actual allowable costs for a particular accounting period will be compensated for by adjusting the rates in a subsequent accounting period.

E. NOTIFICATION TO FEDERAL AGENCIES: Copies of this document may be provided to other Federal agencies as a means of notifying them of the agreement contained herein.

F. SPECIAL REMARKS: None.

BY THE STATE/LOCALITY

By the Cognizant Negotiation Agency On Behalf of the Federal Government

John H. Carrington   /s/

Department of Health, Education & Welfare
Agency

John H. Carrington
Name

Truman P. Burrus   /s/

Comptroller
Title

Truman P. Burrus
Name

March 30, 1976
Date

Ass't. Reg. Director for Fin. Mgmt.
Title

April 7, 1976
Date

Negotiated by   Harry D. Giles

Telephone   (216) 742-0651

204

Appendix 5. Carry-Forward Computation: Department/Agency Indirect Cost Proposal

Source. OASC–10, pp. 82–83.

EXHIBIT B

SAMPLE FORMAT

CARRY-FORWARD COMPUTATION*
DEPARTMENT/AGENCY INDIRECT COST PROPOSAL
DEPARTMENT X

	Initial Year	Subsequent Years	
	FY 1974 (4)	FY 1976 (4)	FY 1978 (4)
(a) Fixed Rate Per Negotiation Agreement (A ÷ B) — Computed as follows:	10.0%	11.4%	9.4%
Direct S&W Base (1)	$4,932,675(B)	$4,938,795(B)	$4,880,450(B)
Indirect Cost Pool:			
Departmental Costs (1)	$470,123	$503,285	$458,745
Department's Share of Central Service Costs (2)	23,144	27,930	35,281
Carry-Forward	-0-	32,549	(37,147)
Total Pool	$ 493,267(A)	$ 563,764(A)	$ 456,879(A)
(b) Actual Costs Negotiated Computed as follows:			

	FY 1974	FY 1976	FY 1978
Actual Direct S&W Base (3)	$4,938,795	$4,880,450	$5,100,100
Actual Indirect Cost Pool:			
Departmental Costs (3)	$503,285	$458,745	$486,270
Department's Share of Central Service Costs (2)	23,144	27,930	35,281
Carry-Forward	-0-	32,549	(37,147)
Total Pool	$ 526,429	$ 519,224	$ 484,404

(c) Carry-Forward Computation:

Recovered:

Fixed Rate × Actual Direct S&W Base

	FY 1974	FY 1976	FY 1978
10.0% × $4,938,795	$ 493,880(E)		
11.4% × $4,880,450		$ 556,371(E)	
9.4% × $5,100,100			$ 479,409(E)

Should Have Recovered:

Actual Indirect Costs For:

	FY 1974	FY 1976	FY 1978
FY 1974	526,429(F)		
FY 1976		519,224(F)	
FY 1978			484,404(F)
Underrecovery (F–E) – Carry-Forward to Subsequent Year	$ 32,549	$ 37,147	
Overrecovery (E–F) – Carry-Forward to Subsequent Year			$ 4,995

*This is a sample only and is not intended to prescribed methods of charging costs.

DEPARTMENT/AGENCY INDIRECT COST PROPOSAL

NOTES

(1) In this illustration, the direct salary and wage base amounts and the departmental indirect cost amounts used for purposes of computing fixed rates, were predicated on actual amounts incurred in a previous year (viz. FY 72 actual costs were used as FY 74 costs). A grantee organization may use more current information for fixing rates, where that information is available, and where in the opinion of the Federal negotiator, the data available is adequate and reasonable. Generally, however, most grantees prefer using historical data.

(2) These amounts were based on an approved State/local central service cost allocation plan which is summarized below. The cost allocation plan should not be submitted with the departmental carry-forward computation; it has been shown here merely to illustrate the source of this data in the departmental carry-forward computation. In most instances the carry-forward adjustment for central service costs is contained as part of the amount currently assessed each Department for central services and the Department need not be concerned with it.

CENTRAL SERVICE COSTS ALLOCATED
TO DEPARTMENT X

	FY 1974		FY 1976		FY 1978	
Fixed Amount	$23,144		$25,537		$30,409	
Add (Deduct) Carry-Forward	-0-		2,393		4,872	
Total Fixed Amount		$23,144		$27,930		$35,281
Actual Amount	$25,537		$30,409		$28,779	
Add (Deduct) Carry-Forward	-0-		2,393		4,872	
Total Actual Amount		25,537		32,802		33,651
Carry-Forward		$ 2,393		$ 4,872		$(1,630)

(3) Based on actual costs for the FY's 74, 76, and 78. These costs are normally known soon after the completion of each of these respective fiscal years, and are obtained from the grantee's records and reflected in the indirect cost proposals submitted to and approved by the cognizant Federal negotiator.

(4) A second cycle would be initiated for the odd number years (i.e., FY 75, 77, and 79) similar to the cycle illustrated above for the even numbered years. The initial year of the odd numbered years would be FY 75. The FY 75 fixed rate computation would be negotiated prior to the beginning of FY 75, would not include a carry-forward amount in the computation of the fixed amount, and would probably use FY 73 actual costs as a basis for fixing FY 75 costs.

(5) The sample above illustrates a department with a single indirect cost rate. Rather than use a single indirect cost rate, some departments will develop multiple rates, i.e., a separately computed indirect cost rate for each division in the department. The same procedures should be followed for a department or agency for which more than one rate is developed, except that a separate carry-forward amount must be computed for every division. The department's share of central service costs and share of departmental indirect costs will have been distributed to each division to arrive at divisional indirect cost rates, so that no special treatment needs to be accorded these costs on a divisional rate basis that has not already been stated for the single rate basis.

208

Appendix 6. Central Service Allocation Plan: Costs to Be Allocated, Personnel Department

Source. OASC–10, p. 51.

COSTS TO BE ALLOCATED; PERSONNEL DEPARTMENT

SCHEDULE A-2

SAMPLE FORMAT*

CENTRAL SERVICE COST ALLOCATION PLAN
COSTS TO BE ALLOCATED, PERSONNEL DEPARTMENT
FOR THE FISCAL YEAR ENDED JUNE 30, 19 --

Salaries and Wages		$140,000
Fringe Benefits		16,000
Supplies		8,000
Travel		7,012
Maintenance & Janitorial Services		7,928
Capital Outlay		7,561
		$186,501
Less: Unallowable Costs, Capital Outlay	$ 7,561	
Costs Chargeable to Federal Grant (b)	30,000	37,561
Total Costs to be allocated on Schedule A-1		$148,940 (a)

(a) The costs allocated must be reconciled to appropriate financial documents, either financial statements, budgets or a combination of both. In this example the government's base data was cost incurred for its most recent fiscal year.

(b) Represents charges to a Federal grant awarded to assist the State or local government to improve its personnel system. If a supporting agency received an award from the Federal Government, all costs incurred in connection with the award (including any costs that are required for matching or cost sharing) must be eliminated prior to the distribution of the supporting agency's costs to the user departments or agencies.

---

*This is a sample only and hence, is brief and simple. In practice, this schedule should be sufficiently detailed to show the costs of major activities, branches, etc. of the personnel departments in a manner permitting a reasonable assessment of the costs claimed against Federal programs.

Appendix 7.
Alternative Method of Cost Allocation

This guide recommends the selective allocation of central service agency costs to other central service agencies, if the services provided to the agencies are in significant amounts. An alternative to a selective allocation is the "step-down" method described in this appendix. This method allocates costs of central service agencies to all departments they serve, including other central service agencies. However, once the costs of a central service agency have been allocated, that agency will receive no allocations from other agencies. "Step-down" refers to the graphic display of the process in which each step of

Table 7-A Example City Central Service Cost Allocation

	1	2	3	4	6	7
	Total for Allocation	Computer Services	Purchas-ing	Finance	Building O and M	City Manager
Central Service Agencies						
1 Computer services	29,560	(29,560)				
2 Purchasing	58,184	—	(58,184)			
3 Finance: Accounting	85,333	11,824	352	(97,509)		
4 Building operation and maintenance	263,625	1182	1114	2417	(268,338)	
5 City manager	56,257	—	183	637	2029	(59,106)
6 Management and budget	55,297	—	1173	1146	5837	827
7 Personnel	83,365	591	528	896	5192	649
8 Printing and mail	17,495	—	163	637	3985	408
9 Telephone	49,099	—	233	256	553	219
10 Garage	330,972	1478	33,231	4442	5755	3053
11 Community relations	21,480	—	176	256	602	177
12 Public information	54,396	591	528	893	1288	591
Operating Agencies						
13 Mayor and council		—	331	725	4588	—
14 Boards and commissions		—	—	60	—	—
15 City attorney		—	195	391	—	112
16 Fire		—	586	16,185	33,211	11,583
17 Police		1774	1173	20,233	63,225	11,695
18 Civil defense		—	519	85	5410	—
19 Communications		—	1466	4063	4509	2840
20 Recorder's court		—	—	212	—	—
21 Public works		2365	6568	29,924	9016	19,874
22 Parks and recreation		—	5278	6883	63,488	3749
23 Community development and planning		—	3812	5812	6762	2611
24 Airport		—	222	663	50,631	266
25 Tax collection and clerk		9755	353	693	2257	452
26 Total	1,105,063	0	0	0	0	0

Plan—Summary of Costs: Step-Down Method of Cost Allocation

8 Management and Budget	9 Personnel	10 Printing and Mail	11 Telephone	12 Garage	13 Community Relations	14 Public Information	15 Total Allocation
							0
							0
							0
							0
							0
(64,280)							0
617	(91,838)						0
438	648	(23,774)					0
176	318	—	(50,854)				0
3055	4853	378	544	(387,761)			0
176	282	314	623	833	(24,919)		0
614	940	2996	1022	1070	272	(65,201)	0
498	—	223	329	—	—	554	7248
41	—	488	—	—	—	46	635
269	178	640	440	—	51	300	2576
11,131	18,410	511	7165	19,193	5332	12,388	135,695
13,883	19,027	7917	14,073	89,994	5383	15,452	263,829
58	—	1036	223	953	—	64	8348
2794	4513	—	300	1332	1357	3110	26,284
146	—	198	—	—	—	163	719
20,722	31,422	1391	6253	248,122	9148	22,906	407,711
4733	5958	2782	7037	18,114	1844	5268	125,134
3997	4150	3338	12,510	6474	1202	4035	54,703
456	422	150	—	1676	122	509	55,117
476	717	1412	335	—	208	406	17,064
0	0	0	0	0	0	0	1,105,063

the allocation distributes costs to one less agency. See Table 7-A.

As with the selective allocation method, the order in which the allocations are made is important. The central service agency providing services to the greatest number of other central service agencies and receiving services from the fewest number of other agencies should be the first to be allocated. After the allocation order is determined, the central service agencies are listed in that order in the left column and across the top of the allocation summary schedule, as shown in Table 7-A. Also, the operating agencies are listed in the left column below the central service agencies. Then for each column, the allocation is made to each agency listed below the one being allocated on the basis of the allocation units. For Example, the Finance Department's costs are entered as a negative number in column 4, row 3, and then allocated to central service agencies on rows 4 through 12 and to all operating agencies.

The problem with this method is that the determination of the allocation order requires very arbitrary decisions. For example, the Personnel Department and City Manager's Office benefit all agencies and both have the allocation basis of "number of personnel." Which one should be allocated first? As another example, the rule just described for determining the order would have computer services allocated last, because it only benefits five central service agencies. However, placing Computer Services last would be a problem, since its principal users are those five agencies. Computer Services' costs must be allocated before Finance, Public Information, Personnel, Garage, and Building Operations and Maintenance. The step-down method is effective for a hospital or another nonprofit organization in which a rational allocation order may be determined by applying this rule. However, for a local government such as the one illustrated in Table 7-A, the decision of which agency's services are received by the greatest number of other agencies is entirely arbitrary, because the Finance, Personnel, Management and Budget, City Manager's Office, and other agencies provide services to all other local government agencies.

Appendix 8. Central Service Costs Allocation Plan: Allocation of Costs, Personnel Department

Source. OASC–10, p. 50.

Allocation of Costs, Personnel Department

SCHEDULE A-1

SAMPLE FORMAT*

CENTRAL SERVICE COST ALLOCATION PLAN
ALLOCATION OF COSTS, PERSONNEL DEPARTMENT
FOR THE FISCAL YEAR ENDED JUNE 30, 19 - -

Department/Unit	Number of Employees (a)	Percent	Allocation (c)
Health	188	6.61	$ 9,945
Environmental Services	170	5.98	8,907
Social Services	61	2.14	3,187
Highway	289	10.16	15,132
Police	570	20.04	29,848
Fire	475	16.70	24,873
Other Departments (b)	1,091	38.37	57,048
Total	2,844	100.00	$148,940

(a)   Allocation base must include all employees of all operating departments that are serviced by the personnel department.

(b)   Those departments that do not perform Federal programs may be grouped together.

(c)   Allocated amounts are carried forward to summary schedule in Exhibit A. The total of $148,940 comes from Schedule A-2.

---

*This is a sample only and, accordingly, is brief and simple. In practice, the type and level of service provided by the personnel department to the various organizations served may require a separate allocation for each service or to different organizations served.

Appendix 9. Department of Environmental Services Indirect Cost Rate Proposal—Short Form Method

Source. OASC–10, p. 54.

DESCRIPTION OF EXHIBIT B

Exhibit B illustrates the computation of indirect costs for programs operated within a department using the short form method. The costs of the department are categorized as indirect costs, direct costs (salaries and wages and other) and expenditures not allowable. The short-form method is the least complex of the various methods of computing departmental indirect cost rates. This method is used in those instances where indirect costs at the division or bureau level are not identified. Thus, all costs incurred at the division or bureau level are treated as direct costs. If division or bureau level indirect costs can be identified, the simplified method (Exhibit C), the alternate simplified method (Exhibit D) or the multiple rate method (Exhibit E) may be used.

EXHIBIT B

SAMPLE FORMAT

DEPARTMENT OF ENVIRONMENTAL SERVICES
INDIRECT COST RATE PROPOSAL–SHORT FORM METHOD*
FOR THE FISCAL YEAR ENDED JUNE 30, 19 - -

	Total Costs Incurred (a)	Excludable Costs (b)	Unallowable Costs (c)	Direct Costs Salaries & Wages (d)	Other	Indirect Costs
Divisions/Bureaus						
Air Quality and Noise	$2,158,100	$1,800,000	$ 21,900	$ 260,100	$ 76,100	
Community Environmental Control	245,200		12,200	187,800	45,200	
Water Quality Management	255,400		9,600	196,700	49,100	
Solid Waste Disposal	642,300		51,000	476,100	115,200	
Parks and Forests	283,700		11,500	216,300	55,900	
Departmental Indirect Costs						
Office of the Director	35,600		1,000			$ 34,600
Financial Management	56,000					56,000
Administrative Services	61,100		500			60,600
Equipment Use	1,000					1,000
Central Service Cost Allocation Plan(e)						
Personnel	8,907					8,907
Accounting	21,622					21,622
Purchasing	2,221					2,221
Audit	1,221					1,221
Total Costs	$3,772,371	$1,800,000	$107,700	$1,337,000	$341,500	$186,171

Rate Calculation

$$\frac{\text{Indirect Costs}}{\text{Direct Salaries and Wages}} \quad \frac{\$ \ 186,171}{\$1,337,000} = 13.92\%$$

*This is a sample only and is not intended to prescribe methods of charging costs.

COST RATE PROPOSAL—SHORT FORM METHOD

Notes to Exhibit B

(a) Total departmental costs. This amount should be reconciled to the financial statements or other supporting documentation submitted with the proposal and would include costs billed from the Central Plan as well as departmental billed costs (Billed costs should be in compliance with Exhibit A-1).

(b) Under some Federal programs funds are provided to a grantee and subsequently passed through to another organization which actually performs the program for which the funds are provided. There is no measurable involvement by the grantee in the use or administration of the funds. This example illustrates such a situation. Since these funds, which are recorded as a cost in the records of the department do not reflect the expenditure of resources, they are excluded from the computation. However, if the grantee does in fact incur a significant amount of costs in administering the grant, then it should be assessed for its equitable share of indirect costs. This column would be normally used by States only and not by local governments.

(c) Expenditures not allowable. This amount represents costs of capital expenditures and other costs which are unallowable under FMC 74-4. Unallowable costs must be allocated their share of indirect costs if they either generated or benefited from the indirect costs. In this example this is not the case.

(d) Salaries and wages. This amount is set out simply because it is the base upon which the indirect cost rate is calculated.

(e) Central Service Cost Allocation Plan Costs. The amounts shown as allocated must agree with the amounts shown on the Central Service Cost Allocation Plan (see Exhibit A.)

Appendix 10. Department of Environmental Services Indirect Cost Rate Proposal—Simplified Method

Source. OASC–10, p. 56.

COST RATE PROPOSAL—SIMPLIFIED METHOD

DESCRIPTION OF EXHIBIT C

Exhibit C illustrates the distribution of indirect costs of a State or local government department, the division/bureaus of the department and the cost of central services provided to it. Exhibit C differs from Exhibit B in that recognition is given to the indirect costs within each division. Under the Short Form Method illustrated in Exhibit B, where indirect costs are not identified at the division or bureau level, all costs are treated as direct costs. Under the Simplified Method shown in this Exhibit, indirect costs are identified at the division or bureau level, and are so indicated. This method may be used if the ratio of the indirect costs to direct salaries and wages (or other selected base) of each division or bureau reasonably approximates the ratio of the other divisions or is otherwise not inequitable to the Federal government. If, the indirect/direct ratio varies significantly between divisions or bureaus, the Alternate Simplified Method (Exhibit D) or the Multiple Rate Method (Exhibit E) should be used.

EXHIBIT C

SAMPLE FORMAT

DEPARTMENT OF ENVIRONMENTAL SERVICES
INDIRECT COST RATE PROPOSAL—SIMPLIFIED METHOD*
FOR THE FISCAL YEAR ENDED JUNE 30, 19 - -

					Direct Costs (c)	
					Direct	Expenditures
			Expenditures		Salaries	For All Other
			Not	Indirect	Salaries	For All Other
	Total	Exclusions	Allowable	Costs	& Wages	Purposes
	(e)	(a)	(b)	(d)		
Division/Bureau						
Air Quality and Noise	$2,149,100	$1,800,000	$ 21,900	$ 28,100	$ 235,400	$ 63,700
Community Environmental Control	245,200		12,200	20,100	170,000	42,900
Water Quality Management	255,400		9,600	21,000	178,100	46,700
Solid Waste Disposal	642,300		51,000	50,900	431,000	109,400
Parks and Forests	283,700		11,500	23,200	195,900	53,100
	$3,575,700	$1,800,000	$106,200	$143,300	$1,210,400	$315,800
Departmental Indirect Costs						
Office of the Director	35,600			35,600		
Financial Management	56,000			56,000		
Administrative Services	62,100			62,100		
Equipment Use	9,000			9,000		
	$3,738,400	$1,800,000	$106,200	$306,000	$1,210,400	$315,800
Services Furnished (But Not Billed)						
By Other Government Agencies (f)						
Personnel	8,907			8,907		
Accounting	21,622			21,622		
Purchasing	2,221			2,221		
Audit	1,221			1,221		
	$3,772,371	$1,800,000	$106,200	$339,971	$1,210,400	$315,800

222

Notes to Exhibit C

(a) Under some Federal programs funds are provided to a grantee and subsequently passed through to another organization actually performs the program for which the funds are provided. There is no measurable involvement by which the grantee in the use of administration of the funds. This example illustrates such a situation. Since these funds, which are recorded as a cost in the records of the department do not reflect the expenditure of resources, they are excluded from the computation. However, if the grantee does in fact incur a significant amount of costs in administering the grant, then it should be assessed for its equitable share of indirect costs. This column is normally used by States only and not local governments.

(b) Expenditures not allowable. This amount represents costs or capital expenditures and costs, whether direct or indirect, which are unallowable in accordance with the cost principles. Although a cost may be unallowable if it either generated or benefited from the indirect costs, it should be moved to the base (providing it is salaries and wages in this example) and allocated its share of indirect costs.

(c) Under the Simplified Method, a determination is made as to which activities are direct, illustrates under the heading Direct Costs, and which are indirect, illustrated under the heading Indirect Costs.

(d) Once the determination of direct/indirect has been made, a ratio should be determined for each division/bureau as shown in the following calculation:

Division/Bureau	Indirect Costs	Direct Salaries and Wages	Ratio
Air Quality & Noise	$28,100	$235,400	11.94%
Community Environmental Control	20,100	170,000	11.82%
Water Quality Management	21,000	178,100	11.79%
Solid Waste Disposal	50,900	431,000	11.81%
Parks & Forests	23,200	195,900	11.84%

In this illustration, the dollar amounts of indirect costs differ significantly between division or bureaus; however, when individually expressed as a percentage of direct salaries and wages the differences are minor. Therefore, a single overall rate for the department may be computed by adding the departmental indirect costs and the costs incurred by other government agencies and allocating the indirect cost pool over a single base.

(e) Total departmental costs. This amount should be reconciled to the financial statements or other supporting documentation included in the proposal.

(f) Costs incurred by other government agencies. This amount must agree with the amounts shown on the central service Cost Allocation Plan (see Exhibit A.) In this illustration, costs of $33,971 represents costs of central services allocated to the entire department. Government-wide services that are billed directly to departments or to programs must also be documented in the cost allocation plan (See Exhibit A-1).

---

*This is a sample only and is not intended to prescribe methods of charging costs.

COST RATE PROPOSAL—SIMPLIFIED METHOD

DESCRIPTION OF EXHIBIT C-1

The totals from Exhibit C are brought forward to this Exhibit. The indirect cost rate is expressed as a percentage resulting from the ratio of the allowable indirect costs ($339,971) to the direct salaries and wages ($1,210,400.)

EXHIBIT C-1

SAMPLE FORMAT

DEPARTMENT OF ENVIRONMENTAL SERVICES
INDIRECT COST RATE PROPOSAL–SIMPLIFIED METHOD*
FOR THE FISCAL YEAR ENDED JUNE 30, 19 - -

Total	Exclusions & Expenditures Not Allowable	Indirect Costs	Direct Salaries & Wages	Other Direct Expenditures
$3,772,371	$1,906,200	$339,971	$1,210,400	$315,800
		(A)	(B)	

(A) divided by (B) = $\dfrac{\$\ 339,971}{\$1,210,400}$ = Indirect cost rate of 28.09% of direct salaries and wages excluding fringe benefits.

Treatment of Fringe Benefits

In this example, fringe benefits applicable to direct salaries and wages are treated as direct costs.

---

*This is a sample only and is not intended to prescribe methods of charging costs.

224

Appendix 11. Department of Environmental Services Indirect Cost Rate Proposal—Alternate Simplified Method

Source. OASC–10, p. 59.

EXHIBIT D

SAMPLE FORMAT

INDIRECT COST RATE PROPOSAL-ALTERNATE SIMPLIFIED METHOD*
DEPARTMENT OF ENVIRONMENTAL SERVICES
FOR THE FISCAL YEAR ENDED JUNE 30, 19- -

	Totals (g)	Exclusions (f)	Departmental Indirect Costs	Allocation To Divisions/ Bureaus	Air Quality and Noise	Community Environmental Control	Water Quality	Solid Waste Disposal	Parks and Forests
							Division/Bureaus		
Expenditures Not Allowable (a)	$ 106,200				$ 21,900	$ 12,200	$ 9,600	$ 51,000	$ 11,500
Direct Salaries and Wages (b)	1,164,700				251,500	178,000	184,700	375,000	175,500
Other Direct Expenditures (b)	2,097,700	$1,800,000			63,700	42,900	46,700	98,400	46,000
Division/Bureau Indirect Costs (b)	207,100				12,000	12,100	14,400	117,900	50,700
Departmental Indirect Costs									
Office of the Director			$ 35,600						
Financial Management			56,000						
Administrative Services			62,100						
Equipment Use			9,000						
Total Departmental Indirect Costs (c)	162,700		162,700	($162,700)	35,133	24,865	25,801	52,385	24,516
Total Departmental Costs	$3,738,400	$1,800,000			$ 384,233	$ 270,065	$ 281,201	$ 694,685	$ 308,216

Services Furnished (But Not Billed) By Other Government Agencies (d)

Personnel	$	8,907
Accounting		21,622
Purchasing		2,221
Audit		1,221

	Total	Air Quality and Noise	Community Environmental Control	Water Quality	Solid Waste Disposal	Parks and Forest
Total Services Furnished (But Not Billed) By Other Government Agencies (d)	($ 33,971)	$ 7,336	$ 5,192	$ 5,387	$ 10,937	$ 5,119
Total Costs	$3,772,371 $1,800,000	$ 391,569	$ 275,257	$ 286,588	$ 705,622	$ 313,335
Total Indirect Costs (e)	$ 403,771	$ 54,469	$ 45,588	$ 45,588	$ 181,222	$ 80,335

Indirect Cost Rates (See Note (e))

	Indirect Costs (c)	Salary and Wages (b)	Ratio
Air Quality and Noise	$ 54,469	$ 251,500	21.66%
Community Environmental Control	42,157	178,000	23.68%
Water Quality	45,588	184,700	24.68%
Solid Waste Disposal	181,222	375,000	48.33%
Parks and Forest	80,335	175,500	45.77%
Total	$403,771	$1,164,700	

*This is a sample only and is not intended to prescribe methods of charging costs.

COST RATE PROPOSAL—ALTERNATE SIMPLIFIED METHOD

Notes to Exhibit D

(a) Expenditures not allowable. This amount represents costs of capital expenditures and both direct and indirect costs which are unallowable in accordance with the cost principles. Although a direct cost may be unallowable, it should be allocated its share of indirect costs if it either generated or benefited from the indirect costs.

(b) A determination is made as to which functions are direct and which are indirect at the division or bureau level. Next, direct salaries and wages are separately identified from other direct expenditures. An analysis is made to determine the ratio of indirect costs to direct salaries and wages to determine the amount of variance between divisions and bureaus:

Division/Bureau	Divisional Indirect Costs	Direct Salaries and Wages	Ratio
Air Quality and Noise	$ 12,000	$ 251,500	4.77%
Community Environmental Control	12,100	178,000	6.80%
Water Quality	14,400	184,700	7.80%
Solid Waste Disposal	117,900	375,000	31.44%
Parks and Forests	50,700	175,500	28.89%
Totals	$207,100	$1,164,700	17.78%

The difference in the rates of indirect costs incurred per division or bureau when related to the direct salaries and wages are significant enough to preclude the use of a single department-wide rate. Separate pools should be established for each division or bureau and a portion of the central service costs and departmental indirect costs allocated to each pool.

(c) In this example, departmental indirect costs are allocated to the division or bureaus on the basis of direct salaries and wages incurred in each division or bureau.

	Direct Salaries and Wages	Percent of Total	Departmental Indirect Costs	Allocated Amount
Air Quality and Noise	$ 251,500	21.6%	$162,700	$ 35,133
Community Environmental Control	178,000	15.3%	162,700	24,865
Water Quality	184,700	15.8%	162,700	25,801
Solid Waste Disposal	375,000	32.2%	162,700	52,385
Parks and Forests	175,500	15.1%	162,700	24,516
Totals	$1,164,700	100.0%		$162,700

(d) Costs incurred by other governmental agencies are allocated to the divisions or bureaus on the basis of direct salaries and wages.

	Direct Salaries and Wages	Percent of Total	Departmental Indirect Costs	Allocated Amount
Air Quality and Noise	$ 251,500	21.6%	$ 33,971	$ 7,336
Community Environmental Control	178,000	15.3%	33,971	5,192
Water Quality	184,700	15.8%	33,971	5,387
Solid Waste Disposal	375,000	32.2%	33,971	10,937
Parks and Forests	175,500	15.1%	33,971	5,119
Totals	$1,164,700	100.0%		$ 33,971

Notes to Exhibit D (Continued)

(e) Total indirect costs include (1) division/bureau indirect costs (2) departmental indirect costs, and (3) services furnished (but not billed) by other government agencies. The total indirect expenses for each division or bureau are carried forward to Exhibit D, where the relationship between the indirect expenses and the direct salaries and wages of each division or bureau is used to develop indirect cost rates.

(f) Under some Federal programs, funds are provided to a grantee and subsequently passed through to another organization which actually performs the program for which the funds are provided. There is no measurable involvement by the grantee in the use or administration of the funds. This example illustrates such a situation. Since these funds, which are recorded as a cost in the records of the department do not reflect the expenditure of resources, they are excluded from the computation. However, if the grantee does in fact incur a significant amount of costs in administering the grant, then it should be assessed for its equitable share of indirect costs. This column would be normally used by States only and not by local governments.

(g) This amount should be reconciled to the financial statements or other supporting documentation submitted with the proposal.

COST RATE PROPOSAL—ALTERNATE SIMPLIFIED METHOD

DESCRIPTION OF EXHIBIT D

This method illustrates the distribution of indirect costs to functional divisions or bureaus in order to determine separate indirect cost rates for each division or bureau. This method provides more definitive costing in those instances where, indirect effort at the division or bureau level is material in amount and differs sufficiently from division to division to warrant a more precise method of costing than shown in the simplified method in Exhibit C.

This computation recognizes indirect costs of (1) each division or bureau, (2) the department, and (3) services furnished (but not billed) by other local government agencies. Indirect costs at the department level and central service level are allocated to the divisions or bureaus on a single base. A rate is then developed for each of the divisions or bureaus by relating the indirect costs of each division or bureau to the selected basis for allocation for each division or bureau.

Appendix 12. Department of Environmental Services Indirect Cost Rate Proposal—Multiple Rate Method

Source. OASC–10, p. 63.

COST RATE PROPOSAL—MULTIPLE RATE METHOD

DESCRIPTION OF EXHIBIT E

Exhibit E illustrates the distribution of indirect costs on a multiple allocation basis to each division or bureau within a Department. This method results in more definitive costing and is for use when operating differences between divisions or bureaus result in material differences in the use of resources and in costs.

The computation recognizes (1) the indirect costs of each division or bureau, (3) department level administration, and (3) the cost of services furnished by other government agencies and approved through the central service cost allocation plan. These costs are allocated to the divisions or bureaus on bases which most fairly give effect to the extent to which they benefit from or generate the costs. For example, the costs of purchasing services is allocated on the number of purchase orders issued while the costs of personnel administration is allocated on the number of employees serviced.

Indirect costs allocated from the department level and from the central service plan are added to the indirect costs incurred by each division or bureau to arrive at total indirect costs for each of the divisions or bureaus. As in the method described in Exhibit D, a rate is developed for each division or bureau by relating its indirect costs to its salaries and wages or other selected base.

232

EXHIBIT E

SAMPLE FORMAT

DEPARTMENT OF ENVIRONMENTAL SERVICES
INDIRECT COST RATE PROPOSAL-MULTIPLE RATE METHOD*
FOR THE FISCAL YEAR ENDED JUNE 30, 19--

	Allocation Base (a)	Total Indirect Costs (b)	Services Furnished by Other Gov't Agencies (c)				Equipment	Departmental Costs (d)			Total (g)
			Personnel	Accounting	Purchasing	Audit		Financial Mgmt.	Admin. Services	Director	
Services Furnished (But Not Billed) By Other Government Agencies (c)											
Personnel	Number of Employees	$ 8,907	($8,907)								
Accounting	Number of Employees (f)	21,622		($21,622)							
Purchasing	Number of Purchase Orders	2,221			($2,221)						
Audit	Number of Audit Hours	1,221				($1,221)					
Subtotal		$ 33,971									
Departmental Indirect Costs											
Equipment Use	User of Equipment	$ 9,000					(9,000)				
Financial Mgmt.	Transaction Processed	56,000						(56,000)			
Admin. Services	Direct Salaries & Wages	62,100							($62,100)		
Director's Office	Direct Salaries & Wages	35,600								($35,600)	
Subtotal		$162,700									
Division/Bureau											
Air Quality & Noise		$ 28,100	$ 1,692	$ 4,108	$ 333	$ 98	$ 200	$ 8,960	$11,799	$ 6,764	$ 62,054
Environ. Control		20,100	1,246	3,027	333	98	400	11,200	8,694	4,984	50,082
Water Quality		21,000	1,157	2,811	222	98	400	8,960	8,694	4,984	48,326
Solid Waste Disposal		50,900	3,562	8,649	1,111	610	7,200	15,120	21,735	12,460	121,347
Parks & Forest		23,200	1,157	2,811	155	195	800	8,400	9,936	5,696	52,350
Plant Construction		15,200	93	216	67	122	-0-	3,360	1,242	712	21,012
Subtotal		$158,500									
Totals		$355,171	-0-	-0-	-0-	-0-	-0-		-0-	-0-	$355,171

*This is a sample only and is not intended to prescribe methods of charging costs.

233

COST RATE PROPOSAL—MULTIPLE RATE METHOD

Notes to Exhibit E

(a) The allocation bases used were selected as reasonable and applicable under the circumstances. Other basis could be just as acceptable if they represented a fair measure of cost generation or cost benefit.

(b) The costs in this column must be reconciled to official financial statements. In this illustration, it is assumed that all costs incurred are allowable and relevent in accordance with FMC 74-4. To the extent that unallowable or excludable (See Exhibit B Note (b)) costs are included therein, a separate column should be added to the schedule to show the amounts and adjustments made.

(c) The costs of services furnished (but not billed) by other government agencies which are derived through the central service cost allocation plan, are allocated to each functional division or bureau. This allocation could be made more precise by allocating the costs to each departmental administrative function e.g., to financial management, administrative services, etc., and to the divisions or bureaus. The indirect costs of each departmental administrative service plus its allocated amount of central service costs would then be allocated to the divisions or bureaus. If the result of such allocations would have a material effect on the rates computed, the more precise method should be used. In the example presented, the dollar effect is not sufficiently material to warrant this level of precision.

(d) Departmental indirect costs are allocated to each division or bureau. As with services furnished by other Federal agencies, explained in Note (c), the allocation of certain departmental indirect costs, such as equipment use charges could have been allocated to other departmental administrative functions, if the results of such allocation would have had a material effect on the rates to be computed. In the example presented, the dollar effect is not sufficiently material to warrant the additional allocations.

(e) The costs of services furnished (but not billed) by other government agencies is derived from the central service cost allocation plan shown in Exhibit A. In addition to the listed unbilled services, the department also received services from other organizations for which it is billed at rates approved through the central service cost allocation plan (See Exhibit A-1). This illustration assumes that these billed costs are already recorded in the accounting records of the department and included in the column—total indirect costs, or treated as a direct cost.

(f) Accounting services rendered by other agencies are allocated to the divisions or bureaus on the basis of number of employees. In this illustration, the accounting services provided by the central service agency were predominently payroll services.

(g) The total indirect expenses developed for each division or bureau is carried forward to Exhibit E-1, where the relationship between the indirect expenses and direct salaries and wages of each division or bureau is used to develop indirect cost rates.

Cost Rate Proposal—Multiple Rate Method

EXHIBIT E-1

SAMPLE FORMAT

DEPARTMENT OF ENVIRONMENTAL SERVICES
INDIRECT COST RATE PROPOSAL-MULTIPLE RATE METHOD
FOR THE FISCAL YEAR ENDED JUNE 30, 19--

Divisions/Bureaus	Indirect Costs (a)	Direct Salaries and Wages (b)	Indirect Cost Rates (a) ÷ (b) (c)
Air Quality and Noise	$ 62,054	$ 225,815	27.48%
Community Environmental Control	50,082	166,390	30.10%
Water Quality Management	48,326	166,390	29.04%
Solid Waste Disposal	121,347	415,975	29.17%
Parks and Forests	52,350	190,160	27.53%
Plant Construction	21,012	23,770	88.40%
	$355,171	$1,188,500	

(a) The amounts in this column are from Exhibit E.
(b) The amounts in this column are derived from and must be reconciled to the books and records of the department. Salaries and wages is the preferred base. However other bases may be used where it results in a more equitable allocation of costs. Generally, the same base should be used for all divisions, however, if approved by the cognizant Federal agency, different bases may be used for one or more of the divisions.
(c) The indirect cost rate for each division/bureau is computed by dividing the indirect costs for each division/bureau by the direct salaries and wages of that division/bureau.

Index